Theory of Knowledge

John W. Yolton
YORK UNIVERSITY

$150

Sources in Philosophy

A MACMILLAN SERIES
Lewis White Beck, General Editor
THE MACMILLAN COMPANY, NEW YORK
COLLIER–MACMILLAN LIMITED, LONDON

THE MACMILLAN COMPANY, NEW YORK

COLLIER-MACMILLAN CANADA, LTD., TORONTO, ONTARIO

Printed in the United States of America

Contents

Introduction

The purpose of this Introduction is twofold. It is first of all to introduce the reader to an area of philosophy which he may not have encountered before. The terminology and the problems in theory of knowledge will sound strange and be obscure to such a reader. The selections included in this anthology might serve by themselves as a sufficient introduction were it not that they have all been torn from an historical and (in most cases) polemical context. To fill in that context in detail would be to present the history of the subject. Short of that—and such is the rationale for this volume—the editor can provide some indication of the contexts and the issues involved as a means of easing the reader into this area of philosophy.

The second purpose of this Introduction is to attempt to reveal some of the excitement of the debates in theory of knowledge by suggesting where these debates stand in the contemporary scene. Philosophy in general is, I think, best studied by allowing the historical study to shed light upon contemporary disputes, and by allowing contemporary disputes to interpret the historical analyses. We must, of course, always be on guard against anachronism, but the significance and continuing importance of philosophical problems can best be appreciated if we can find some contemporary foothold in terms of which these problems remain significant for us. In short, it is intellectually healthy to look to the forefront òf contemporary philosophical debates for our understanding of particular areas of philosophy, while never permitting the contemporary idiom to define for us those areas.

The study of the history of philosophy discloses, what the label itself suggests, that what has come to be called "theory of knowledge" (also "philosophy of knowledge" and "epistemology") marks a concern with questions about knowing and knowledge. A companion label is "theory of reality," a designation for concerns with questions about the nature of the world and of man. This area of theory of reality (usually termed "metaphysics"), it is sometimes said, is the more fundamental of the two. Aristotle called it the study of "being *qua* being," that is, the study of what there is and of the properties of what there is. But of course, any account of the world or of man ought to have some backing; the metaphysician writing fantasy or the scientist composing science fiction does not

1

command our attention. We would like to have their credentials to enable us to judge the worth of what they say about man and the world. Questions about knowing and knowledge arise at this point: Can the account of the world and of man be defended as a knowledge-claim? How, in fact, do we come to know anything at all?

If I say "I know that the table is made of oak," I am advancing a claim for which you expect me to have reasons which I ought to be able to defend and explain. Such a claim states more than the locution, "I believe the desk is made of oak," though the belief-claim too has some grounds and some defense. Theory of knowledge is in part concerned with the relations between claims and reasons, with the different sorts of reasons which can serve to back up any knowledge-claim or belief-claim. The interest in the claims and reasons for claiming what we do claim constitute what I am calling the *normative* or *justificatory* aspects of theory of knowledge. To know requires not only that I have reasons which will justify my knowing and my claim; it requires as well that I be aware, that I have perceived, understood, inferred, weighed evidence, etc. The analysis of these various sorts of mental operations—of perceiving, understanding, inferring, etc.—comprises what I am calling *descriptive* epistemology.

Descriptive and normative frequently shade into each other, but the history of philosophy reveals both sorts of concern in theory of knowledge. The selections which follow fall into three divisions focusing around this descriptive-normative contrast.

Part I—*Descriptive Epistemology*, being the interest in describing how awareness first arises and what mental operations unfold in leading us to knowledge. The concern here is also with characterizing these operations as *mental*.

Part II—*Some Forms of Cognition*, being an analysis of particular processes, e.g., of believing, remembering, and of making predictions, as instances of mental operations requisite for knowledge. The essays in this part will be found to be both descriptive and normative, though more the latter than the former.

Part III—*Normative Epistemology*, being the attempt to find criteria of knowledge which cannot be questioned, as well as the attempt to reject the possibility of such criteria.

PART I—DESCRIPTIVE EPISTEMOLOGY

Aristotle reminds us that all men by nature desire to know. He then proceeds to indicate the various stages in awareness which lead up to and make knowledge possible. Obviously, one of the conditions for knowledge is a sentient organism, with an intact brain and nervous system. It is not these conditions for knowledge, however, that Aristotle talks about. His analysis ignores neurophysiology and concentrates upon the mental operations of knowing. He saw a development and progress in these operations, a development both genetic and logical. Thus, we find him insisting upon the order: sensation, memory, experience, art, and reasoning. Just as we would today distinguish between the physical processes in the brain and nervous system and stimuli for those processes, so Aristotle distinguished between the mental processes and their contents, their objects. Correlated with the scale of mental operations of sensing, remembering, etc., he cited three types of objects: sense-impressions, particular objects like tables and chairs, and universals or class properties shared by many particular objects. Knowledge proper for him has to do with universals, class characteristics, e.g., "man," not "this particular man." Aristotle's teacher, Plato, made similar distinctions between mental processes and the objects or contents of these processes; his account was set forth in the divided-line and cave analogies in his *Republic*.

Locke also talked in genetic terms about the emergence and growth of awareness. What he called the "plain, historical method" attempted to characterize how, in fact, sensing, perceiving, attending, judging, and considering function in supplying the mind with the data for knowledge. Locke was also careful to distinguish the physical processes leading up to awareness (causal operations by tiny corpuscles) from the resulting awareness. He left the details of the causal processes to science. His *Essay Concerning Human Understanding* was a detailed account of our mental processes. Locke did argue that all mental processes, and all the objects of these processes, were derived from sensation and reflection. He was confuting what he took to be a false doctrine, one which claimed that some mental contents were innate, not derived from the physical world via sensation. His concern to refute such a doctrine led him to give most of his attention to sensation and reflection, though, in his accounts of these processes and their contents, Locke relied heavily upon many other mental operations.

An important aspect of all such mental operations and their contents is the factor of *significance,* or *meaning.* When we respond to our friend's request to do this or that, when we follow traffic signals and signs in driving, when we guide ourselves through a forest, we are reacting to stimuli. But so are we reacting to stimuli (or stimuli are being reacted to) when our eyes blink at oncoming objects. The processes within our bodies are also reactions to stimuli, e.g., when light waves are translated into electrical impulses in the nerve tissue of eye and brain. The differences between these various stimuli and reactions to them (e.g., light as an electromagnetic radiation and light as sensed in our awareness) have not always been emphasized. The importance of these differences emerges when we wish to give an account of those responses to stimuli which not only are learned responses—very few responses are unaffected by learning—but which require attention, understanding, and conscious awareness. The epistemologist interested in describing knowing in the broad sense of conscious awareness frequently finds himself meeting the psychologist attempting to deal with similar topics. Before the explicit development of a discipline called "psychology," the philosopher had to work alone in his attempts at describing the cognitive processes. Even so, many philosophers did not stress the importance of meaning and significance in the cognitive response.

The notion of meaning can, of course, be employed in such a way that the differences between the eye-blink, the activities of neurons, my unselfconscious reactions to stimuli as I move about, and my responses to oral requests and to the written word are blurred or denied. The epistemologist will follow this course only at great risk, for in doing so he is close to denying cognition entirely, or to interpreting cognition in terms of some electronic or mechanical model. There is room for argument here, to be sure; but before the advantage of a common model for all reactions to stimuli overpowers us with its explanatory force, it is wise to examine carefully the case for differences in kind. Not only does Cassirer draw a sharp line between electronic, mechanical, and physical reactions to stimuli but he also insists, even more strongly, upon the difference in kind between animal and human behavior. His analysis of the learning experiences of Helen Keller gives a forceful case for singling out man's psychological responses as unique.

In one sense the difference is obvious, though many philosophers and psychologists often talk as if they were denying or underplaying the difference. Cassirer is careful to present the development of awareness from physiological to psychological response. What is presented briefly in the selection included in this anthology, from his *Essay on Man*, is elaborated in some of his other writings. He has termed his analysis "philosophical anthropology." Another more recent label for the sort of analysis he offers is "philosophical psychology." Descriptive epistemology leads to such overlapping of disciplines just because it is concerned with exploring the nature and operations of mental processes. The overlap, however, of philosophy and psychology is not so marked as it might seem. One of the more important issues in contemporary theory of knowledge is the question of whether we can or should talk at all about mental processes. Philosophers and psychologists have recently tended to ignore the mental aspects of knowing. Psychologists concentrate upon behavior or neurophysiology, primarily because the physical processes of the body (both overt and internal) can be observed, experiments can be devised, and conclusions can be checked by approved scientific methods. Philosophers have been caught in a bind. Recognizing that they can add little by way of information to the study of man and his world, pressed on all sides by the advance of particular sciences, the contemporary philosopher has found a way of talking about the world in an indirect fashion. He talks about the world by talking about language, about the use of words, just those words essential for talking about thinking, knowing, believing, etc. An analysis of the language of morals, for instance, still talks about traditional problems of ethics, but what is said is said via an examination of ethical speech, by watching the roles of such words as "good," "right," "duty." [1] Another important contemporary book, *The Concept of Mind*, by G. Ryle, talks about mind, thinking, and perceiving by analyzing mental conduct words and giving what Ryle calls their "logical geography," i.e., locating them in relation to other kinds of words which behave in other ways.

[1] R. M. Hare, *The Language of Morals* (New York: Oxford University Press, 1952).

Concern with being very scientific on the one hand, and concern to avoid being scientific at all on the other, have tended to lead psychologist and philosopher respectively to overlook the analysis of thinking, believing, knowing, etc., as cognitive processes. Some of the more traditional philosophers, not affected by this contemporary dispute, have attempted to address themselves to the substantive questions here. Contemporary philosophical psychology is just beginning to return to those questions.

PART II — SOME FORMS OF COGNITION

While a major problem in descriptive epistemology is that of characterizing the differences and connections between physiological and psychological reactions to stimuli, another important task is that of distinguishing the various sorts of mental processes at work in cognition, and getting clear about their order. Two orders have been followed by philosophers of knowledge. The one order is genetic and chronological; the philosopher must be aided here by science. There are difficulties, inherent in the subject matter of such genetic analysis, which introduce an element of speculation into the account, namely, the difficulties of knowing what awareness is like for the early infant or for primitive man. Contributions to such genetic analysis have been made by biologists, neurologists, animal psychologists, psychoanalysts, learning theorists, and philosophers. The philosopher is more inclined to resort to the second order of cognition, the logical order. For this order, he takes the sophisticated theories and claims of science as the terminus, or goal, of other modes of cognition. Clearly, the infant does not theorize. Likewise, it is reasonable to observe that sensing and the use of memory must precede the use of judgment. There are, in short, some obvious priorities in chronology which fit into a logical ordering. Some forms of cognition are necessary for other forms.

A philosopher's attention to the particular forms of cognition slides easily between a descriptive and a normative interest; which interest is paramount in some particular writer is not always obvious. But usually, when a philosopher gives an analysis of some form of cognition, he has purposes in mind other than that of describing that form of cognition. Thus, Russell's interest in perception (p. 47) arises not only from what seems an obvious point—that knowledge of a physical world must come through our sensory organs—but also from Russell's belief about the nature of the physical world which he wishes to protect in his account of perception. Russell's analysis of perception is also controlled by criteria he accepts for knowledge, criteria of certainty which were voiced by Descartes. The theory of knowledge and the theory of reality are especially intertwined in Russell's account of perception. He is not unique in this respect. Philosophers of knowledge have frequently been obsessed with saying what there is; they have tried to move from knowing to being. Thus we find proofs for an external world based upon the features of sensing or perception, proofs for other minds constructed upon what we know in our own case and what we are aware of beyond ourselves. The philosopher has sometimes rushed through his analysis of knowing in order to see what, on the basis of that analysis, we are justified in saying there is. Some of the controversy in theory of knowledge has arisen because one of the parties to the dispute has failed to notice that the other is talking on the justificatory, not the factual level. Disputes over the analysis of perception are noteworthy in this respect. What some perception theorists say is not what *in fact* we see, but rather what, given specific criteria of knowledge and belief about reality, we are *entitled to say* we see. That is, the philosopher of knowledge is not concerned with the facts of perception or learning, with adding to our stock of information about these processes. Even when he is engaged in what I am calling descriptive epistemology, the philosopher's goal is not just the description of such processes; he frequently describes only as a means of dealing with some normative problem. Readers are sometimes astonished at the things philosophers write; often this astonishment can be dissipated if they understand this distinction between what there is and what we can say there is.

To the reader approaching Russell for the first time, it may seem ludicrous for Russell to say we do not see physical objects. What it is we are said to see, and the way in which such seeing is related to the world which Russell wants to say is there, are important points typical of the philosophical analysis of perception. The normative control enters in the way in which the account of perception is a function of prior commitments to a criterion of knowledge and a theory of reality. To know, in *that* sense, that sort of world, requires *that* sort of account of perception.

The accounts of some of our forms of cognition are thus frequently controlled by presuppositions about the nature of knowing or of the objects known. In other cases, the analysis of some cognitive process is urgent because of the role that process plays in assessing the trustworthiness of other such processes. For example, suppose our memory were always false, that we always misremembered. Memory functions in recognitions (even in the most elementary and genetically earliest recognition), in retrodiction of the past, and in predictions of the future. If memory plays us short, we may believe and say our claims are true while not being entitled so to believe or so to say. If memory-knowledge cannot be justified, no knowledge-claims can be trusted. Price elaborates the arguments for this point in his essay on memory-knowledge, though in a later work [2] he has suggested that for recognition (in the early, genetic sense) correct memory may not be necessary. Recognition would seem to require two conditions: (1) regularities in the world and (2) repeated stimuli upon the living organism from those regularities. Price's suggestion in the book cited above is that condition (1) is not necessary, that recognition requires only a feeling of familiarity, not regularities in the world. Recognition as a conscious experience is thus viewed as distinct from the further question of the truth-reference of that experience. Price does not want to suggest that the whole of our experience and knowledge is built upon a feeling which cannot itself be trusted, but only that that feeling is a sufficient condition for conscious recognition.

This distinction between memory as *feeling* and memory as *trusted source of information about the past* may seem to open the door to scepticism, to a distrust of all memory. Russell has suggested that our cognitive experiences could be as they are, even though the world had been created just minutes ago, complete with men making memory-claims, having evidence-bearing documents, etc.[3] Such a condition would be deception on a grand scale, on such a scale that most philosophers deny this possibility, or at least the meaningfulness of this supposition. There are important truths on the side of Russell's supposition, but there are, as well, truths on the side of those who argue against the possibility of a total mistrust of memory. We cannot, of course, remember a past that never was, though we can make mistakes in what we claim to

[2] H. H. Price, *Thinking and Experience* (London: Hutchinson, 1953), p. 51.
[3] Bertrand Russell, *The Analysis of Mind* (London, 1921), pp. 159–160.

remember. Why cannot we, then, make a mistake in all our memory-claims, especially if the reality-condition (i.e., no past at all) is such as to make all knowledge-claims of past events impossible? We need to notice that there would be a difference in kind between the persons living in the world supposed by Russell asking this question about all memory and *our* questioning Russell's supposition. The persons living in such a truncated world would have no way of suspecting anything unusual. In fact, they could not doubt all knowledge, since this is to make a knowledge-claim. The statement "I doubt . . ." expresses a truth which Descartes insists upon, that is, that I know at least that I am doubting, and I cannot be wrong about that. But to express a doubt, like expressing a belief, can be justified only if we have some grounds which we know to be true, as Price (p. 59) points out. That is, it does not make sense to doubt *all* memories, for the only reason we have to doubt *any* memory is that one memory (or set of memories) gives us reason to doubt some memory-claim that is not consonant with it. If we rejected all of our memories, we would reject the only reason we have for rejecting any of them.

Yet it is worth noting that Russell's supposition is meaningful: we can see what it would be like were those conditions fulfilled, though we could not know whether or not they were fulfilled without, as it were, being on the outside of any such world. If in claiming that this object is the same object I saw yesterday, I have made a mistake, I may never discover this mistake. My claim may be founded on a belief, even, as Price says, on a feeling that this is the same object or the same experience. If in making a claim about past events I am in error, I may never discover the error if the evidence I have seems to me to warrant what I claim. The condition for making memory-claims is not that I have reasons for trusting the memory: having the memory is sufficient for advancing the claim. Price's essay on memory-knowledge in this volume is concerned with the justification of memory. In the book cited above, his remarks about memory as feeling are directed towards the causes of memory-claims. This distinction between the *causes* of memory-claims and the *reasons* which will justify them is another version of the difference between descriptive and normative epistemology.

Not only do we make claims about the past, we also have expectations about the future and we predict events yet to occur. A justificatory question arises here also: What right do we have for trusting our predictions? Our predictions are based upon the regularities we have found. Some regularities are obvious and taken for granted, like chairs supporting our weight; others have to be carefully discovered, like those in astronomy. Because we have found events in the past standing in significant correlations, we are naturally led to expect those correlations to occur again. We would be shocked, for example, if we went up in the air when we stepped down the stairs. Our world, even our awareness, is built upon such regularities. The philosopher does not deny these expectations of future regularities, but he does ask about the justification of such expectations. As in the case of memory-knowledge, so in that of inductive-knowledge, two different questions arise. The one question concerns our everyday inferences from past experience to present generalizations or predictions about future events. The other question seeks for a justification, in general, for so inferring and predicting. More specifically, Hume wants to know whether the principle that the future will be like the past can be justified. This question is tied in with what is meant by "justification." Hume says that a cause is not necessary for every event because it is possible to conceive of some event now occurring without also conceiving of a cause for that event. What Hume seems to understand by "conceive" is not a psychological, but a logical operation. In brief, the possibility of an event not having a cause, the possibility of the future not being like the past, are logical possibilities: we can deny causes of events and we can deny that the future will be like the past without involving ourselves in a logical contradiction. That is, the statement "X is an event without a cause" and the statement "the sun will not rise tomorrow" are not self-contradictory statements as "Jones is a bachelor and married" is self-contradictory.

To justify induction might mean to show that statements of this sort (about specific future events) or statements of the more general sort ("the future will be like the past") are logical truths whose denial is self-contradictory. But such an interpretation of "justify" would be much too stringent. Another possible meaning for the phrase "to justify induction" would be to show that there are deductive relations between statements about past regularities and statements about future regularities. While this claim is less stringent than the preceding one, it seems a hopeless claim, since at best only a person with omniscient knowledge would be in a position to make *deductions* of future events from past events. Still a third way of explaining Hume's remarks about induction is to say he showed that we cannot *know* that the future will be like the past, we can only *believe* it will be. He *was* much occupied with belief, his analysis of induction and causation is made in close connection with his analysis of belief. Hume was one of the first philosophers to call attention to the importance of belief for theory of knowledge. In this anthology, Price's essay on belief gives a good account of the differences between belief and knowledge, between the locutions "I believe that P" and "I know that P." But this contrast between belief and knowledge requires an understanding of the very special sense of "knowledge" which pervades much of normative epistemology.

PART III — NORMATIVE EPISTEMOLOGY

Knowledge, as opposed to conjecture or belief, has had a particular fascination for the philosopher. Frequently he claims access to a special sort of knowing which gives him insight into the nature of the world. The history of philosophy has many examples of philosophers recommending various sorts of formulae for achieving the special insight which they identify with knowledge. Sometimes the formula calls for intuition, preceded by special training; at other times knowledge is seen as arising through aesthetic experiences. Other writers, being more inclined toward reason than toward intuition, have claimed that reason itself can, when properly employed, lead to special insights into the world. The partisan of reason insists upon criteria for knowledge which are not as subjective as are appeals to intuition, to the "natural light of reason," or to innate truths.[4]

If I am working in an apple orchard and I am told by the foreman to sort these apples into eating apples and cider apples (those to be pressed into juice), the criteria I am to use may be obvious. But the foreman, in order to be sure of my performance, may call my attention to the characteristics of cider apples. I could carry out his instruction by watching carefully for the cider apple characteristics. When I begin work, I do not know the difference between eating apples and cider apples. With a knowledge of

[4] The appeal to intuition, to the "natural light of reason," and to innate truths was common in the sixteenth and seventeenth centuries.

the criteria of the latter sort, I now know the difference. Are we ever in a similar situation about knowledge itself, such that ignorance is replaced by knowledge in virtue of our being supplied with criteria?

Descartes tried to search for knowledge by feigning ignorance of everything save a criterion of knowledge. His criterion was not clearly formulated until after he had, through doubt, discovered a statement which could not be doubted; but the implicit criterion for determining when a statement or belief could not be doubted was a logical criterion. Certain knowledge, a statement which cannot be doubted, would be such that its denial would be self-contradictory. He then proceeded to examine various candidates purporting to satisfy this criterion. There is much debate about whether Descartes did produce an instance of certain knowledge: he thought that the proposition "I am, I exist" was a proposition whose truth is certain when one utters that proposition. To say (and mean it) "I do not exist" is, if not self-contradictory, at least odd. Descartes was unable to obtain any further truths without adding dubious assumptions to the "I am, I exist" proposition. It is very doubtful whether anything more than the proposition about one's own existence can be obtained by means of Descartes' experiment in doubt, although there is a parallel example found in Russell's essay, the certainty of immediate awareness. Chisholm's "non-comparative appear statements" (p. 103) embody a similar certainty. These propositions of immediate awareness can be given various formulations, the safest being something like "I am being appeared to in a table-like way." When we separate what *is* from what *appears to · be*, we can then assert, with a certainty akin to that of Descartes' proposition, a proposition about appearances to a subject. But just as Descartes cannot make any other moves without extra assumptions, so Russell's starting point of an indubitable proposition about appearances can serve no epistemological function by itself: it must be helped out by *ad hoc* assumptions.

The ideal of a knowledge whose certainty is such that we cannot be in error about it has served as a standard for many in theory of knowledge. Even philosophers like Locke and Hume who urge us to derive all cognitive claims from sense experience, measured such sensory knowledge by the standard of deductive, logically certain knowledge. Those who have confronted Descartes' claim of having solved the problem of the criterion by establishing criteria from the very experience which produced an instance satisfying the criterion, have reacted in several different ways. There are three main reactions: (1) there is Chisholm's rejection, not of criteria, but of the stringent Cartesian criteria and of the way such criteria were established; (2) there is Arner's rejection of the legitimacy of asking for criteria at all; and (3) there is the sceptic's rejection of the possibility of justifying knowledge, of finding instances which satisfy the knowledge criteria.

In one sense, Chisholm denies that there can be a criterion, a mark of evidence which, prior to having any evidence, will indicate when we come across some evidence, when we do have some knowledge. Chisholm questions the propriety of asking "what is knowledge?" while pretending we do not have in our possession bits of knowledge. If we do not already know what counts as knowledge, how can we recognize the knowing which is knowledge? There are parallels in ethics. If we do not already know, in some sense of "know," which actions are morally right and wrong, we are hardly in a position to go out in the world looking for right actions. Aristotle's answer to the moral question "how do we learn which actions are right?" is that we acquire such "knowledge" through habit and custom instilled by our family and society. Chisholm's solution to the problem of the criterion runs along similar lines: we "know" beforehand what the marks of evidence are, what we take as valid knowledge-claims. As he remarks in his book on perception, "when we set out to solve the problem of the criterion, we already knew which propositions are the ones that are evident; we knew in advance that skepticism with regard to the senses is mistaken." [5] The task for theory of knowledge is then to formulate these marks, to make them explicit. In the selection included in this anthology, Chisholm attempts to formulate a satisfactory criterion for our perceptual knowledge, what he calls "the sensibly taking criterion." The decision as to what sort of criterion to formulate was made by considering what it is we want to say we know in perception; "I see a cat on the roof" becomes the paradigm for perceptual claims.

Opposed to the quest for criteria which will delineate knowledge, no matter where or when it is found, Arner stresses the contextual nature of knowledge-claims. As he says in the essay included in this volume, "What counts as conclusive evidence is a matter of

[5] Roderick M. Chisholm, *Perceiving: A Philosophical Study* (Ithaca, N. Y.: Cornell University Press, 1957), p. 102.

tacit, continuing agreement among the users of the language." The philosopher cannot stand apart from society and proclaim special earmarks of knowledge in general. What we claim to know must be so, but the grounds for making the claim are found in the context of assertion, in the subject matter and circumstances. The grounds for scientific claims differ from those for more ordinary, less technical claims. Arner agrees with Chisholm that there cannot be a mark of evidence for evidence; the authorities for knowledge-claims cannot be queried indefinitely.

Another feature of Arner's essay worth noticing is the way he catches the sceptic using the logical criteria of knowledge. Like the philosopher who claims a special sort of insight, the sceptic uses the word "knowledge" to designate a very special type of cognition, a type which cannot be wrong, which lacks even the possibility of being wrong. The sceptic assumes that before we can know that S is P it must be impossible that S is not P, and "impossible" is used in the logical sense employed by Descartes and Hume. That is, something is "possible" if its denial is not self-contradictory; "impossible" if it is self-contradictory. The sceptic offers still other kinds of considerations designed to cast doubt upon any knowledge-claim. Sometimes the sceptic has in mind the fact that further experiences may force us to revise our claims, but always the unattainable ideal of knowledge which is logically sound in all its phases hovers in the background of the sceptic's case. One of the classic statements of the sceptic's case is found in Hume's *Enquiry Concerning Human Understanding.* Hume himself recommends a "mitigated scepticism" which recognizes some of the points Chisholm and Arner later urged. The final selection of this anthology contains portions of Hume's statement.

CONCLUSION

The reader of this anthology will discover that the selections follow the pattern which I have indicated in this Introduction. The first group of essays is primarily concerned with ways in which the materials for cognition arise and reach consciousness as significant data. The second group of essays probes into some specific ways of organizing these materials into perceptual objects, memory objects, or objects of belief. The ways of structuring the data of cognition into these sorts of objects also come in for their share of analysis.

Hovering in the background of the analysis of some specific forms of cognition is the worry about justifying these modes of knowing. This question about justification in the third group of essays has its particular and general aspects: Can this specific memory-claim or belief-claim be trusted? Can any memory or belief be known to be true? The generalized "problem of the criterion" for knowledge arises when the philosopher keeps belief distinct from knowledge, reserving for knowledge the characteristic of being true and incapable of being false. But a knowledge-claim which is both true and incapable of being false may not be known to be true and incapable of being false. The quest for a criterion which will serve as a signal telling us when we do have knowledge of this sort has been for some philosophers of knowledge the ultimate goal of analysis. Whether this goal can be reached, whether it would be of any use if reached, and in what sense we can and cannot have such an ultimate criterion are questions which the final part of this anthology explores.

The reader should realize that once he has worked his way through these selections and understood the problems which they raise, he is then in a position to follow them out in more detail. The brief bibliography appended at the end of this volume can serve as an initial guide for further reading in theory of knowledge.

PART I

Descriptive Epistemology

ARISTOTLE

On Knowing

Aristotle (384–322 B.C.). Greek philosopher and student of Plato. He was also the teacher of Alexander the Great and founder of a school in Athens in 335 B.C. He is said to have lectured on many subjects and to have written many books for publication. All that are extant, however, are what appear to be lecture notes on logic, metaphysics, physics, psychology, ethics, poetics, and political theory.

I

All men by nature desire to know. An indication of this is the delight we take in our senses; for even apart from their usefulness they are loved for themselves; and above all others the sense of sight. For not only with a view to action, but even when we are not going to do anything, we prefer seeing (one might say) to everything else. The reason is that this, most of all the senses, makes us know and brings to light many differences between things.

By nature animals are born with the faculty of sensation, and from sensation memory is produced in some of them, though not in others. And therefore the former are more intelligent and apt at learning than those which cannot remember; those which are incapable of hearing sounds are intelligent though they cannot be taught,

From *The Complete Works of Aristotle,* trans. W. D. Ross (New York: Random House, 1947). Used by permission of the Clarendon Press, Oxford. Section I is taken from *Metaphysics,* Bk. I, Chap. 1, pp. 980a–981b; Section II is taken from *Posterior Analytics,* Bk. II, Chap. 19, pp. 99b–100b.

e.g. the bee, and any other race of animals that may be like it; and those which besides memory have this sense of hearing can be taught.

The animals other than man live by appearances and memories, and have but little of connected experience; but the human race lives also by art and reasonings. Now from memory experience is produced in men; for the several memories of the same thing produce finally the capacity for a single experience. And experience seems pretty much like science and art, but really science and art come to men *through* experience; for 'experience made art', as Polus says,[1] 'but inexperience luck'. Now art arises when from many notions gained by experience one universal judgement about a class of objects is produced. For to have a judgement that when Callias was ill of this disease this did him good, and similarly in the case of Socrates and in many individual cases, is a matter of experience; but to judge that it has done good to all persons of a certain constitution, marked off in one class, when they were ill of this disease, e.g. to phlegmatic or bilious people when burning with fever—this is a matter of art.

With a view to action experience seems in no respect inferior to art, and men of experience succeed even better than those who have theory without experience. (The reason is that experience is knowledge of individuals, art of universals, and actions and productions are all concerned with the individual; for the physician does not cure *man*, except in an incidental way, but Callias or Socrates or some other called by some such individual name, who happens to be a man. If, then, a man has the theory without the experience, and recognizes the universal but does not know the individual included in this, he will often fail to cure; for it is the individual that is to be cured.) But yet we think that *knowledge* and *understanding* belong to art rather than to experience, and we suppose artists to be wiser than men of experience (which implies that Wisdom depends in all cases rather on knowledge); and this because the former know the cause, but the latter do not. For men of experience know that the thing is so, but do not know why, while the others know the 'why' and the cause. Hence we think also that the master-workers in each craft are more honourable and know in a truer sense and are wiser than the manual workers, because they know the causes of the things that are done (we think the manual

[1] Cf. Plato's *Gorgias*, 448C, 462BC.

workers are like certain lifeless things which act indeed, but act without knowing what they do, as fire burns—but while the lifeless things perform each of their functions by a natural tendency, the labourers perform them through habit); thus we view them as being wiser not in virtue of being able to act, but of having the theory for themselves and knowing the causes. And in general it is a sign of the man who knows and of the man who does not know, that the former can teach, and therefore we think art more truly knowledge than experience is; for artists can teach, and men of mere experience cannot.

II

As to the basic premisses [of demonstrations and syllogisms], how they become known and what is the developed state of knowledge of them is made clear by raising some preliminary problems.

We have already said that scientific knowledge [2] through demonstration is impossible unless a man knows the primary immediate premisses. But there are questions which might be raised in respect of the apprehension of these immediate premisses: one might not only ask whether it is of the same kind as the apprehension of the conclusions, but also whether there is or is not scientific knowledge of both; or scientific knowledge of the latter, and of the former a different kind of knowledge; and, further, whether the developed states of knowledge are not innate but come to be in us, or are innate but at first unnoticed. Now it is strange if we possess them from birth; for it means that we possess apprehensions more accurate than demonstration and fail to notice them. If on the other hand we acquire them and do not previously possess them, how could we apprehend and learn without a basis of pre-existent knowledge? For that is impossible, as we used to find [3] in the case of demonstration. So it emerges that neither can we possess them from birth, nor can they come to be in us if we are without knowledge of them to the extent of having no such developed state at all. Therefore we must possess a capacity of some sort, but not such as to rank higher in accuracy than these developed states. And this at least is an obvious characteristic of all animals, for they possess a congenital discrim-

[2] By "scientific knowledge" Aristotle means simply "knowledge of the causes of a thing."—Ed.

[3] *Posterior Analytics*, Bk. I, Chap. 1.

inative capacity which is called sense-perception. But though sense-perception is innate in all animals, in some the sense-impression comes to persist, in others it does not. So animals in which this persistence does not come to be have either no knowledge at all outside the act of perceiving, or no knowledge of objects of which no impression persists; animals in which it does come into being have perception and can continue to retain the sense-impression in the soul: and when such persistence is frequently repeated a further distinction at once arises between those which out of the persistence of such sense-impressions develop a power of systematizing them and those which do not. So out of sense-perception comes to be what we call memory, and out of frequently repeated memories of the same thing develops experience; for a number of memories constitute a single experience.[4] From experience again—i.e. from the universal now stabilized in its entirety within the soul, the one beside the many which is a single identity within them all—originate the skill of the craftsman and the knowledge of the man of science, skill in the sphere of coming to be and science in the sphere of being.

We conclude that these states of knowledge are neither innate in a determinate form, nor developed from other higher states of knowledge [by *deduction*], but from sense-perception. It is like a rout in battle stopped by first one man making a stand and then another, until the original formation has been restored. The soul is so constituted as to be capable of this process.

Let us now restate the account given already, though with insufficient clearness. When one of a number of logically indiscriminable particulars has made a stand, the earliest universal [5] is present in the soul: for though the act of sense-perception is of the particular, its content is universal—is man, for example, not the man Callias. A fresh stand is made among these rudimentary universals, and the process does not cease until the indivisible concepts, the true universals, are established: e.g. such and such a species of animal is a step towards the genus animal, which by the same process is a step towards a further generalization.

Thus it is clear that we must get to know the primary premisses by induction; for the method by which even sense-perception im-

[4] Cf. *Metaphysics*, A 980a.

[5] As Aristotle goes on to explain, the term "universal" refers to "class"; the difference between "the man Callias" and "man" is the difference between the particular and universal.—Ed.

plants the universal is inductive. Now of the thinking states by which we grasp truth, some are unfailingly true, others admit of error—opinion, for instance, and calculation, whereas scientific knowing and intuition are always true: further, no other kind of thought except intuition is more accurate than scientific knowledge, whereas primary premisses are more knowable than demonstrations, and all scientific knowledge is discursive. From these considerations it follows that there will be no scientific knowledge of the primary premisses, and since except intuition nothing can be truer than scientific knowledge, it will be intuition that apprehends the primary premisses—a result which also follows from the fact that demonstration cannot be the originative source of demonstration, nor, consequently, scientific knowledge of scientific knowledge. If, therefore, it is the only other kind of true thinking except scientific knowing, intuition will be the originative source of scientific knowledge. And the originative source of science grasps the original basic premiss, while science as a whole is similarly related as originative source to the whole body of fact.

JOHN LOCKE

On the Origin of Knowledge

John Locke (1632–1704) was an English philosopher who studied and taught at Oxford. His publications in economics, religion, political theory, and theory of knowledge came late in life. He had an active interest in politics and was himself active (sometimes behind the scene) in the political life of England before and after the revolution of 1688. Besides the work from which this selection is taken, Locke is best known for his political book Two Treatises on Government.

I

1. Every man being conscious to himself that he thinks, and that which his mind is applied about whilst thinking being the *ideas* that are there, it is past doubt that men have in their minds several *ideas* such as are those expressed by the words *whiteness, hardness, sweetness, thinking, motion, man, elephant, army, drunkenness* and others: it is in the first place then to be inquired, how he comes by them? I know it is a received doctrine that men have native *ideas* and original characters stamped upon their minds in their very first being. This opinion I have at large examined already; and, I suppose, what I have said in the foregoing book will be much more easily admitted when I have shown whence the understanding may get all the *ideas* it has, and by what ways and degrees they may come into the mind; for which I shall appeal to everyone's own observation and experience.

2. Let us then suppose the mind to be, as we say, white paper void of all characters, without any *ideas*. How comes it to be furnished? Whence comes it by that vast store which the busy and boundless fancy of man has painted on it with an almost endless variety? Whence has it all the materials of reason and knowledge? To this I answer, in one word, from *experience;*[1] in that all our knowledge

From Locke's *Essay Concerning Human Understanding*, ed. John W. Yolton (Everyman's Library; London: J. M. Dent & Sons Ltd., 1961), Bk. II, Chap. I, Secs. 1–8 [Sec. I in this anthology]; Bk. II, Chap. IX, Secs. 2–15 [Sec. II]. Used by permission of Dent and of E. P. Dutton & Co., Inc., New York.

[1] The reader should note that Locke's use of the term "experience" tends to

is founded, and from that it ultimately derives itself. Our observation, employed either about *external sensible objects, or about the internal operations of our minds perceived and reflected on by ourselves, is that which supplies our understandings with all the materials of thinking.* These two are the fountains of knowledge, from whence all the *ideas* we have, or can naturally have, do spring.

3. First, *our senses,* conversant about particular sensible objects do *convey into the mind* several distinct *perceptions* of things, according to those various ways wherein those objects do affect them. And thus we come by those *ideas* we have of *yellow, white, heat, cold, soft, hard, bitter, sweet,* and all those which we call sensible qualities; which when I say the senses convey into the mind, I mean, they from external objects convey into the mind what produces there those *perceptions.* This great source of most of the *ideas* we have, depending wholly upon our senses, and derived by them to the understanding, I call SENSATION.

4. Secondly, the other fountain from which experience furnisheth the understanding with *ideas* is the *perception of the operations of our own minds* within us, as it is employed about the *ideas* it has got; which operations, when the soul comes to reflect on and consider, do furnish the understanding with another set of *ideas,* which could not be had from things without. And such are *perception, thinking, doubting, believing, reasoning, knowing, willing,* and all the different actings of our own minds; which we, being conscious of and observing in ourselves, do from these receive into our understandings as distinct *ideas* as we do from bodies affecting our senses. This source of *ideas* every man has wholly in himself; and though it be not sense, as having nothing to do with external objects, yet it is very like it, and might properly enough be called internal sense. But as I call the other *sensation,* so I call this REFLECTION, the *ideas* it affords being such only as the mind gets by reflecting on its own operations within itself. By REFLECTION then, in the following part of this discourse, I would be understood to mean that notice which the mind takes of its own operations, and the manner of them, by reason whereof there come to be *ideas* of these operations in the understanding. These two, I say, viz. external material

---

be restricted to sense-experience (though a full reading of his *Essay* will qualify this remark), while Aristotle's use of the same term applies after sensation and memory have done their work.—Ed.

things as the objects of SENSATION, and the operations of our own minds within as the objects of REFLECTION, are to me the only originals from whence all our *ideas* take their beginnings. The term *operations* here I use in a large sense, as comprehending not barely the actions of the mind about its *ideas*, but some sort of passions arising sometimes from them, such as is the satisfaction or uneasiness arising from any thought.

5. The understanding seems to me not to have the least glimmering of any *ideas* which it doth not receive from one of these two. *External objects furnish the mind with the* ideas *of sensible qualities*, which are all those different perceptions they produce in us; and the *mind furnishes the understanding with* ideas *of its own operations*.

These, when we have taken a full survey of them and their several modes, combinations, and relations, we shall find to contain all our whole stock of *ideas*, and that we have nothing in our minds which did not come in one of these two ways. Let anyone examine his own thoughts and thoroughly search into his understanding and then let him tell me whether all the original *ideas* he has there are any other than of the objects of his *senses*, or of the operations of his mind, considered as objects of his *reflection*. And how great a mass of knowledge soever he imagines to be lodged there, he will, upon taking a strict view, see that he has *not any* idea *in his mind but what one of these two have imprinted*, though perhaps, with infinite variety compounded and enlarged by the understanding, as we shall see hereafter.

6. He that attentively considers the state of a *child*, at his first coming into the world, will have little reason to think him stored with plenty of *ideas*, that are to be the matter of his future knowledge. It is by degrees he comes to be furnished with them. And though the *ideas* of obvious and familiar qualities imprint themselves before the memory begins to keep a register of time and order, yet it is often so late before some unusual qualities come in the way, that there are few men that cannot recollect the beginning of their acquaintance with them. And if it were worthwhile, no doubt a child might be so ordered as to have but a very few, even of the ordinary *ideas*, till he were grown up to a man. But all that are born into the world being surrounded with bodies that perpetually and diversely affect them, variety of *ideas*, whether care be taken about it or no, are imprinted on the minds of children. *Light*

and *colours* are busy at hand everywhere when the eye is but open; *sounds* and some *tangible qualities* fail not to solicit their proper senses and force an entrance to the mind; but yet, I think it will be granted easily that, if a child were kept in a place where he never saw any other but black and white till he were a man, he would have no more *ideas* of scarlet or green than he that from his childhood never tasted an oyster or a pineapple has of those particular relishes.

7. Men then come to be furnished with fewer or more simple *ideas* from without, according as the *objects* they converse with afford greater or less variety; and from the operation of their minds within, according as they more or less *reflect* on them. For, though he that contemplates the operations of his mind cannot but have plain and clear *ideas* of them: yet, unless he turn his thoughts that way and consider them *attentively*, he will no more have clear and distinct *ideas* of all the *operations of his mind*, and all that may be observed therein, than he will have all the particular *ideas* of any landscape, or of the parts and motions of a clock, who will not turn his eyes to it and with attention heed all the parts of it. The picture or clock may be so placed that they may come in his way every day, but yet he will have but a confused *idea* of all the parts they are made up of, till he *applies himself with attention* to consider them each in particular.

8. And hence we see the reason why 'it is pretty late before most children get *ideas* of the operations of their own minds; and some have not any very clear or perfect *ideas* of the greatest part of them all their lives. Because, though they pass there continually, yet, like floating visions, they make not deep impressions enough to leave in the mind clear, distinct, lasting *ideas*, till the understanding turns inwards upon itself, *reflects* on its own *operations*, and makes them the object of its own contemplation. Children, when they come first into it, are surrounded with a world of new things which, by a constant solicitation of their senses, draw the mind constantly to them, forward to take notice of new and apt to be delighted with the variety of changing objects. Thus the first years are usually employed and diverted in looking abroad. Men's business in them is to acquaint themselves with what is to be found without; and so growing up in a constant attention to outward sensations, seldom make any considerable reflection on what passes within them, till they come to be of riper years; and some scarce ever at all.

II

2. *What perception is,* everyone will know better by reflecting on what he does himself, when he sees, hears, feels, etc., or thinks, than by any discourse of mine. Whoever reflects on what passes in his own mind cannot miss it. And if he does not reflect, all the words in the world cannot make him have any notion of it.

3. This is certain: that whatever alterations are made in the body, if they reach not the mind; whatever impressions are made on the outward parts, if they are not taken notice of within, there is no perception. Fire may burn our bodies with no other effect than it does a billet, unless the motion be continued to the brain, and there the sense of heat, or *idea* of pain, be produced in the mind; wherein consists *actual perception.*

4. How often may a man observe in himself that, whilst his mind is intently employed in the contemplation of some objects, and curiously surveying some *ideas* that are there, it takes no notice of impressions of sounding bodies made upon the organ of hearing, with the same alteration that used to be for the producing the idea of sound. A sufficient impulse there may be on the organ, but it not reaching the observation of the mind, there follows no perception; and though the motion that used to produce the *idea* of sound be made in the ear, yet no sound is heard. Want of sensation, in this case, is not through any defect in the organ, or that the man's ears are less affected than at other times when he does hear: but that which used to produce the *idea,* though conveyed in by the usual organ, not being taken notice of in the understanding, and so imprinting no *idea* in the mind, there follows no sensation. *So that wherever there is sense or perception, there some* idea *is actually produced, and present in the understanding.*

5. Therefore I doubt not but *children,* by the exercise of their senses about objects that affect them *in the womb, receive some few* ideas, before they are born, as the unavoidable effects either of the bodies that environ them or else of those wants or diseases they suffer; amongst which (if one may conjecture concerning things not very capable of examination) I think the *ideas* of hunger and warmth are two: which probably are some of the first that children have and which they scarce ever part with again.

6. But though it be reasonable to imagine that *children* receive

some *ideas* before they come into the world, yet these simple *ideas* are *far from* those *innate principles* which some contend for and we above have rejected. These here mentioned, being the effects of sensation, are only from some affections of the body which happen to them there, and so depend on something exterior to the mind, no otherwise differing in their manner of production from other *ideas* derived from sense but only in the precedency of time; whereas those innate principles are supposed to be quite of another nature, not coming into the mind by any accidental alterations in or operations on the body, but, as it were, original characters impressed upon it in the very first moment of its being and constitution.

7. As there are some *ideas* which we may reasonably suppose may be introduced into the minds of children in the womb, subservient to the necessities of their life and being there, so after they are born *those* ideas are the *earliest imprinted which happen to be the sensible qualities which first occur* to them; amongst which light is not the least considerable nor of the weakest efficacy. And how covetous the mind is to be furnished with all such *ideas* as have no pain accompanying them may be a little guessed by what is observable in children new-born, who always turn their eyes to that part from whence the light comes, lay them how you please. But the *ideas* that are most familiar at first, being various according to the divers circumstances of children's first entertainment in the world, the order wherein the several *ideas* come at first into the mind is very various and uncertain also; neither is it much material to know it.

8. We are further to consider concerning perception that the *ideas we receive by sensation are often* in grown people *altered by the judgment,* without our taking notice of it. When we set before our eyes a round globe of any uniform colour, v.g. gold, alabaster, or jet, it is certain that the *idea* thereby imprinted in our mind is of a flat circle, variously shadowed, with several degrees of light and brightness coming to our eyes. But we having, by use, been accustomed to perceive what kind of appearance convex bodies are wont to make in us, what alterations are made in the reflections of light by the difference of the sensible figures of bodies: the judgment presently, by an habitual custom, alters the appearances into their causes. So that from that which is truly variety of shadow or colour, collecting the figure, it makes it pass for a mark of figure and frames to itself the perception of a convex figure and an uniform colour, when the *idea* we receive from thence is only a plane variously col-

oured, as is evident in painting. To which purpose I shall here insert a problem of that very ingenious and studious promoter of real knowledge, the learned and worthy Mr. *Molyneux*, which he was pleased to send me in a letter some months since; and it is this: *Suppose a man born blind, and now adult, and taught by his touch to distinguish between a cube and a sphere of the same metal, and nighly of the same bigness, so as to tell, when he felt one and the other, which is the cube, which the sphere. Suppose then the cube and sphere placed on a table, and the blind man to be made to see:* quaere, *whether by his sight, before he touched them, he could now distinguish and tell which is the globe, which the cube?* To which the acute and judicious proposer answers: *Not. For, though he has obtained the experience of how a globe, how a cube affects his touch, yet he has not yet obtained the experience that what affects his touch so or so must affect his sight so or so; or that a protuberant angle in the cube, that pressed his hand unequally, shall appear to his eye as it does in the cube.* I agree with this thinking gentleman, whom I am proud to call my friend, in his answer to this problem; and am of opinion that the blind man, at first sight, would not be able with certainty to say which was the globe, which the cube, whilst he only saw them, though he could unerringly name them by his touch, and certainly distinguish them by the difference of their figures felt. This I have set down and leave with my reader as an occasion for him to consider how much he may be beholding to experience, improvement, and acquired notions, where he thinks he has not the least use of or help from them; and the rather, because this observing *gentleman* further adds that, *having upon the occasion of my book proposed this to divers very ingenious men, he hardly ever met with one that at first gave the answer to it which he thinks true, till by hearing his reasons they were convinced.*

9. But this is not, I think, usual in any of our *ideas*, but those received by *sight*. Because sight, the most comprehensive of all our senses, conveying to our minds the *ideas* of light and colours, which are peculiar only to that sense; and also the far different *ideas* of space, figure, and motion, the several varieties whereof change the appearances of its proper object, viz. light and colours: we bring ourselves by use to judge of the one by the other. This, in many cases by a settled habit, in things whereof we have frequent experience, is performed so constantly and so quick, that we take that for the perception of our sensation which is an *idea* formed by

our judgment; so that one, v¹z. that of sensation, serves only to excite the other, and is scarce taken notice of itself; as a man who reads or hears with attention and understanding, takes little notice of the characters or sounds, but of the *ideas* that are excited in him by them.

10. Nor need we wonder that this is done with so little notice, if we consider how very *quick* the *actions of the mind* are performed; for, as itself is thought to take up no space, to have no extension, so its actions seem to require no time, but many of them seem to be crowded into an instant. I speak this in comparison to the actions of the body. Anyone may easily observe this in his own thoughts, who will take the pains to reflect on them. How, as it were in an instant, do our minds, with one glance, see all the parts of a demonstration, which may very well be called a long one, if we consider the time it will require to put it into words, and step by step show it another? *Secondly,* we shall not be so much surprised that this is done in us with so little notice, if we consider how the facility which we get of doing things by a custom of doing makes them often pass in us without our notice. *Habits,* especially such as are begun very early, come at last to *produce actions in us which often escape our observation.* How frequently do we, in a day, cover our eyes with our eye-lids, without perceiving that we are at all in the dark? Men that by custom have got the use of a by-word do almost in every sentence pronounce sounds which though taken notice of by others they themselves neither hear nor observe. And therefore it is not so strange that our mind should often change the *idea* of its sensation into that of its judgment, and make one serve only to excite the other, without our taking notice of it.

11. This faculty of *perception* seems to me to be that which *puts the distinction betwixt the animal kingdom and the inferior parts of nature.*² For, however vegetables have, many of them, some degrees of motion, and upon the different application of other bodies to them, do very briskly alter their figures and motions, and so have obtained the name of sensitive plants, from a motion which has some resemblance to that which in animals follows upon sensation: yet I suppose it is all bare mechanism, and no otherwise produced than the turning of a wild oat-beard by the insinuation of the par-

---

² This section and the next few sections should be compared with Cassirer's discussion of this same point, the differences between animals and men (see pp. 35–46 in this anthology).—Ed.

ticles of moisture, or the shortening of a rope by the affusion of water. All which is done without any sensation in the subject, or the having or receiving any *ideas.*

12. *Perception,* I believe, is, in some degree, *in all sorts of animals;* though in some possibly the avenues provided by nature for the reception of sensations are so few, and the perception they are received with so obscure and dull, that it comes extremely short of the quickness and variety of sensation which is in other animals; but yet it is sufficient for, and wisely adapted to, the state and condition of that sort of animals who are thus made, so that the wisdom and goodness of the Maker plainly appear in all the parts of this stupendous fabric and all the several degrees and ranks of creatures in it.

13. We may, I think, from the make of an *oyster* or *cockle* reasonably conclude that it has not so many, nor so quick senses as a man or several other animals; nor if it had would it, in that state and incapacity of transferring itself from one place to another, be bettered by them. What good would sight and hearing do to a creature that cannot move itself to or from the objects wherein at a distance it perceives good or evil? And would not quickness of sensation be an inconvenience to an animal that must lie still where chance has once placed it, and there receive the afflux of colder or warmer, clean or foul water, as it happens to come to it?

14. But yet I cannot but think there is some small dull perception whereby they are distinguished from perfect insensibility. And that this may be so, we have plain instances, even in mankind itself. Take one in whom decrepit old age has blotted out the memory of his past knowledge and clearly wiped out the *ideas* his mind was formerly stored with, and has, by destroying his sight, hearing, and smell quite, and his taste to a great degree, stopped up almost all the passages for new ones to enter; or, if there be some of the inlets yet half open, the impressions made are scarce perceived or not at all retained. How far such an one (notwithstanding all that is boasted of innate principles) is in his knowledge and intellectual faculties above the condition of a *cockle* or an *oyster,* I leave to be considered. And if a man had passed sixty years in such a state, as it is possible he might, as well as three days, I wonder what difference there would have been, in any intellectual perfections, between him and the lowest degree of animals.

15. *Perception* then being the *first step and degree towards knowl-*

edge and the inlet of all the materials of it: the fewer senses any man, as well as any other creature, hath; and the fewer and duller the impressions are that are made by them; and the duller the faculties are that are employed about them: the more remote are they from that knowledge which is to be found in some men. But this, being in great variety of degrees (as may be perceived amongst men), cannot certainly be discovered in the several species of animals, much less in their particular individuals. It suffices me only to have remarked here that perception is the first operation of all our intellectual faculties, and the inlet of all knowledge in our minds. And I am apt, too, to imagine that it is perception in the lowest degree of it which puts the boundaries between animals and the inferior ranks of creatures. But this I mention only as my conjecture by the by, it being indifferent to the matter in hand which way the learned shall determine it.

ERNST CASSIRER

Knowing as Symbolizing

Ernst Cassirer (1874–1945) was a German philosopher who taught in Germany, England, and finally in America, where he died. He wrote substantial works in almost every field of philosophy and was especially noted as an historian of philosophy. He was interested in myth and language as well as in the philosophy of science and theory of knowledge. One work in particular, besides that from which the following selection is taken, has influenced contemporary philosophers, his The Philosophy of Symbolic Forms.

The biologist Johannes von Uexküll has written a book in which he undertakes a critical revision of the principles of biology. Biology, according to Uexküll, is a natural science which has to be developed by the usual empirical methods—the methods of observation and experimentation. Biological thought, on the other hand, does not belong to the same type as physical or chemical thought. Uexküll is a resolute champion of vitalism; he is a defender of the principle of the autonomy of life. Life is an ultimate and self-dependent reality. It cannot be described or explained in terms of physics or chemistry. From this point of view Uexküll evolves a new general scheme of biological research. As a philosopher he is an idealist or phenomenalist. But his phenomenalism is not based upon metaphysical or epistemological considerations; it is founded rather on empirical principles. As he points out, it would be a very naïve sort of dogmatism to assume that there exists an absolute reality of things which is the same for all living beings. Reality is not a unique and homogeneous thing; it is immensely diversified, having as many different schemes and patterns as there are different organisms. Every organism is, so to speak, a monadic being. It has a world of its own because it has an experience of its own. The phenomena that we find in the life of a certain biological species are not transferable to any other species. The experiences—and therefore the realities—of two different organisms are incommensurable with one another. In the world of a fly, says Uexküll, we find only "fly things"; in the world of a sea urchin we find only "sea urchin things."

From Ernst Cassirer, *An Essay on Man* (New Haven: Yale University Press, 1944), pp. 41–56. Used by permission of Yale University Press.

From this general presupposition Uexküll develops a very ingenious and original scheme of the biological world. Wishing to avoid all psychological interpretations, he follows an entirely objective or behavioristic method. The only clue to animal life, he maintains, is given us in the facts of comparative anatomy. If we know the anatomical structure of an animal species, we possess all the necessary data for reconstructing its special mode of experience. A careful study of the structure of the animal body, of the number, the quality, and the distribution of the various sense organs, and the conditions of the nervous system, gives us a perfect image of the inner and outer world of the organism. Uexküll began his investigations with a study of the lowest organisms; he extended them gradually to all the forms of organic life. In a certain sense he refuses to speak of lower or higher forms of life. Life is perfect everywhere; it is the same in the smallest as in the largest circle. Every organism, even the lowest, is not only in a vague sense adapted to . . . but entirely fitted into . . . its environment. According to its anatomical structure it possesses a certain *Merknetz* and a certain *Wirknetz*—a receptor system and an effector system. Without the coöperation and equilibrium of these two systems the organism could not survive. The receptor system by which a biological species receives outward stimuli and the effector system by which it reacts to them are in all cases closely interwoven. They are links in one and the same chain which is described by Uexküll as the *functional circle* . . . of the animal.[1]

I cannot enter here upon a discussion of Uexküll's biological principles. I have merely referred to his concepts and terminology in order to pose a general question. Is it possible to make use of the scheme proposed by Uexküll for a description and characterization of the *human world*? Obviously this world forms no exception to those biological rules which govern the life of all the other organisms. Yet in the human world we find a new characteristic which appears to be the distinctive mark of human life. The functional circle of man is not only quantitatively enlarged; it has also undergone a qualitative change. Man has, as it were, discovered a new method of adapting himself to his environment. Between the receptor system and the effector system, which are to be found in all animal species, we find in man a third link which we may describe as the *symbolic*

[1] See Johannes von Uexküll, *Theoretische Biologie* (2nd ed. Berlin, 1938); *Umwelt und Innenwelt der Tiere* (1909; 2nd ed. Berlin, 1921).

system. This new acquisition transforms the whole of human life. As compared with the other animals man lives not merely in a broader reality; he lives, so to speak, in a new *dimension* of reality. There is an unmistakable difference between organic reactions and human responses. In the first case a direct and immediate answer is given to an outward stimulus; in the second case the answer is delayed. It is interrupted and retarded by a slow and complicated process of thought. At first sight such a delay may appear to be a very questionable gain. Many philosophers have warned man against this pretended progress. "L'homme qui médite," says Rousseau, "est un animal dépravé": it is not an improvement but a deterioration of human nature to exceed the boundaries of organic life.

Yet there is no remedy against this reversal of the natural order. Man cannot escape from his own achievement. He cannot but adopt the conditions of his own life. No longer in a merely physical universe, man lives in a symbolic universe. Language, myth, art, and religion are parts of this universe. They are the varied threads which weave the symbolic net, the tangled web of human experience. All human progress in thought and experience refines upon and strengthens this net. No longer can man confront reality immediately; he cannot see it, as it were, face to face. Physical reality seems to recede in proportion as man's symbolic activity advances. Instead of dealing with the things themselves man is in a sense constantly conversing with himself. He has so enveloped himself in linguistic forms, in artistic images, in mythical symbols or religious rites that he cannot see or know anything except by the interposition of this artificial medium. His situation is the same in the theoretical as in the practical sphere. Even here man does not live in a world of hard facts, or according to his immediate needs and desires. He lives rather in the midst of imaginary emotions, in hopes and fears, in illusions and disillusions, in his fantasies and dreams. "What disturbs and alarms man," said Epictetus, "are not the things, but his opinions and fancies about the things."

From the point of view at which we have just arrived we may correct and enlarge the classical definition of man. In spite of all the efforts of modern irrationalism this definition of man as an *animal rationale* has not lost its force. Rationality is indeed an inherent feature of all human activities. Mythology itself is not simply a crude mass of superstitions or gross delusions. It is not merely chaotic, for it possesses a systematic or conceptual form.[2] But, on the other hand, it would be impossible to characterize the structure of myth as rational. Language has often been identified with reason, or with the very source of reason. But it is easy to see that this definition fails to cover the whole field. It is a *pars pro toto;* it offers us a part for the whole. For side by side with conceptual language there is an emotional language; side by side with logical or scientific language there is a language of poetic imagination. Primarily language does not express thoughts or ideas, but feelings and affections. And even a religion "within the limits of pure reason" as conceived and worked out by Kant is no more than a mere abstraction. It conveys only the ideal shape, only the shadow, of what a genuine and concrete religious life is. The great thinkers who have defined man as an *animal rationale* were not empiricists, nor did they ever intend to give an empirical account of human nature. By this definition they were expressing rather a fundamental moral imperative. Reason is a very inadequate term with which to comprehend the forms of man's cultural life in all their richness and variety. But all these forms are symbolic forms. Hence, instead of defining man as an *animal rationale,* we should define him as an *animal symbolicum.* By so doing we can designate his specific difference, and we can understand the new way open to man—the way to civilization.

FROM ANIMAL REACTIONS TO HUMAN RESPONSES

By our definition of man as an *animal symbolicum* we have arrived at our first point of departure for further investigations. But it now becomes imperative that we develop this definition somewhat in order to give it greater precision. That symbolic thought and symbolic behavior are among the most characteristic features of human life, and that the whole progress of human culture is based on these conditions, is undeniable. But are we entitled to consider them as the special endowment of man to the exclusion of all other organic beings? Is not symbolism a principle which we may trace back to a much deeper source, and which has a much broader range of applicability? If we answer this question in the negative we must, as it seems, confess our ignorance concerning many fundamental

[2] See Cassirer, *Die Begriffsform im mythischen Denken* (Leipzig, 1921).

questions which have perennially occupied the center of attention in the philosophy of human culture. The question of the *origin* of language, of art, of religion becomes unanswerable, and we are left with human culture as a given fact which remains in a sense isolated and, therefore, unintelligible.

It is understandable that scientists have always refused to accept such a solution. They have made great efforts to connect the fact of symbolism with other well-known and more elementary facts. The problem has been felt to be of paramount importance, but unfortunately it has very rarely been approached with an entirely open mind. From the first it has been obscured and confused by other questions which belong to a quite different realm of discourse. Instead of giving us an unbiased description and analysis of the phenomena themselves the discussion of this problem has been converted into a metaphysical dispute. It has become the bone of contention between the different metaphysical systems: between idealism and materialism, spiritualism and naturalism. For all these systems the question of symbolism has become a crucial problem, on which the future shape of science and metaphysics has seemed to hinge.

With this aspect of the problem we are not concerned here, having set for ourselves a much more modest and concrete task. We shall attempt to describe the symbolic attitude of man in a more accurate manner in order to be able to contradistinguish it from other modes of symbolic behavior found throughout the animal kingdom. That animals do not always react to stimuli in a direct way, that they are capable of an indirect reaction, is evidently beyond question. The well-known experiments of Pavlov provide us with a rich body of empirical evidence concerning the so-called representative stimuli. In the case of the anthropoid apes a very interesting experimental study by Wolfe has shown the effectiveness of "token rewards." The animals learned to respond to tokens as substitute for food rewards in the same way in which they responded to food itself.[3] According to Wolfe the results of varied and protracted training experiments have demonstrated that symbolic processes occur in the behavior of anthropoid apes. Robert M. Yerkes, who describes these experiments in his latest book, draws from them an important general conclusion.

That they [symbolic processes] are relatively rare and difficult to

[3] J. B. Wolfe, "Effectiveness of Token-rewards for Chimpanzees," *Comparative Psychology Monographs*, 12, No. 5.

observe is evident. One may fairly continue to question their existence, but I suspect that they presently will be identified as antecedents of human symbolic processes. Thus we leave this subject at a
most exciting stage of development, when discoveries of moment
seem imminent.[4]

It would be premature to make any predictions with regard to the
future development of this problem. The field must be left open for
future investigations. The interpretation of the experimental facts,
on the other hand, always depends on certain fundamental concepts
which have to be clarified before the empirical material can bear its
fruit. Modern psychology and psychobiology take this fact into account. It seems to me highly significant that nowadays it is not the
philosophers but the empirical observers and investigators who
appear to be taking the leading roles in solving this problem. The
latter tell us that after all the problem is not merely an empirical
one but to a great degree a logical one. George Révész has recently
published a series of articles in which he starts off with the proposition that the warmly debated question of so-called *animal language*
cannot be solved on the basis of mere facts of animal psychology.
Everyone who examines the different psychological theses and theories with an unbiased and critical mind must come at last to the
conclusion that the problem cannot be cleared up by simply referring to forms of animal communication and to certain animal accomplishments which are gained by drill and training. All such
accomplishments admit of the most contradictory interpretations.
Hence it is necessary, first of all, to find a correct logical starting
point, one which can lead us to a natural and sound interpretation
of the empirical facts. This starting point is the *definition of
speech. . . .*[5] But instead of giving a ready-made definition of
speech, it would be better perhaps to proceed along tentative lines.
Speech is not a simple and uniform phenomenon. It consists of different elements which, both biologically and systematically, are not
on the same level. We must try to find the order and interrelation-
ships of the constituent elements; we must, as it were, distinguish
the various geological strata of speech. The first and most funda-

[4] Robert M. Yerkes, *Chimpanzees, A Laboratory Colony* (New Haven: Yale
University Press, 1943), p. 189.

[5] G. Révész, "Die menschlichen Kommunikationsformen und die sogenannte
Tiersprache," *Proceedings of the Netherlands Akademie van Wetenschappen,*
XLIII (1940), Nos. 9, 10; XLIV (1941), No. 1.

mental stratum is evidently the language of the emotions. A great portion of all human utterance still belongs to this stratum. But there is a form of speech that shows us quite a different type. Here the word is by no means a mere interjection; it is not an involuntary expression of feeling, but a part of a sentence which has a definite syntactical and logical structure.[6] It is true that even in highly developed, in theoretical language the connection with the first element is not entirely broken off. Scarcely a sentence can be found—except perhaps the pure formal sentences of mathematics—without a certain affective or emotional tinge.[7] Analogies and parallels to emotional language may be found in abundance in the animal world. As regards chimpanzees Wolfgang Koehler states that they achieve a considerable degree of expression by means of gesture. Rage, terror, despair, grief, pleading, desire, playfulness, and pleasure are readily expressed in this manner. Nevertheless one element, which is characteristic of and indispensable to all human language, is missing: we find no signs which have an objective reference or meaning. "It may be taken as positively proved," says Koehler, "that their gamut of *phonetics* is entirely 'subjective,' and can only express emotions, never designate or describe objects. But they have so many phonetic elements which are also common to human languages, that their lack of articulate speech cannot be ascribed to *secondary* (glosso-labial) limitations. Their gestures too, of face and body like their expression in sound, never designate or 'describe' objects (Bühler)."[8]

Here we touch upon the crucial point in our whole problem. The difference between *propositional language* and *emotional language* is the real landmark between the human and the animal world. All the theories and observations concerning animal language are wide of the mark if they fail to recognize this fundamental difference.[9] In all the literature of the subject there does not seem

[6] For the distinction between mere emotive utterances and "the normal type of communication of ideas that is speech," see the introductory remarks of Edward Sapir, *Language* (New York: Harcourt, Brace, 1921).

[7] For further details see Charles Bally, *Le langage et la vie* (Paris, 1936).

[8] Wolfgang Koehler, *The Mentality of Apes* (New York: Harcourt Brace, 1925), App., p. 317.

[9] An early attempt to make a sharp distinction between propositional and emotional language was made in the field of the psychopathology of language. The English neurologist Jackson introduced the term "propositional language" in order to account for some very interesting pathological phenomena. He

to be a single conclusive proof of the fact that any animal ever made the decisive step from subjective to objective, from affective to propositional language. Koehler insists emphatically that speech is definitely beyond the powers of anthropoid apes. He maintains that the lack of this invaluable technical aid and the great limitation of those very important components of thought, the so-called images, constitute the causes which prevent animals from ever achieving even the least beginnings of cultural development.[10] The same conclusion has been reached by Révész. Speech, he asserts, is an anthropological concept which accordingly should be entirely discarded from the study of animal psychology. If we proceed from a clear and precise definition of speech, all the other forms of utterances, which we also find in animals, are automatically eliminated.[11] Yerkes, who has studied the problem with special interest speaks in a more positive tone. He is convinced that even with respect to language and symbolism there exists a close relationship between man and the anthropoid apes. "This suggests," he writes, "that we may have happened upon an early phylogenetic stage in the evolution of symbolic process. There is abundant evidence that various other types of sign process than the symbolic are of frequent occurrence and function effectively in the chimpanzee." [12] Yet all this remains definitely prelinguistic. Even in the judgment of Yerkes all these functional expressions are exceedingly rudimentary, simple, and of limited usefulness by comparison with human cognitive processes.[13] The genetic question is not to be confused here with the analytical and phenomenological question. The logical analysis of human speech always leads us to an element of prime importance which has no parallel in the animal world. The general theory of evolution in no sense stands in the way of the acknowledgment of this fact. Even in the field of the phenomena

---

found that many patients suffering from aphasia had by no means lost the use of speech but that they could not employ their words in an objective, propositional sense. Jackson's distinction proved to be very fruitful. It has played an important part in the further development of the psychopathology of language. For details see Cassirer, *Philosophy of Symbolic Forms,* III, chap. vi.

[10] Koehler, *The Mentality of Apes,* p. 277.

[11] Révész, *op. cit.,* XLIII, Part II (1940), 33.

[12] Yerkes and Nissen, "Pre-linguistic Sign Behavior in Chimpanzees," *Science,* LXXXIX, 587.

[13] Yerkes, *Chimpanzees,* p. 189.

of organic nature we have learned that evolution does not exclude a sort of original creation. The fact of sudden mutation and of emergent evolution has to be admitted. Modern biology no longer speaks of evolution in terms of earlier Darwinism; nor does it explain the causes of evolution in the same way. We may readily admit that the anthropoid apes, in the development of certain symbolic processes, have made a significant forward step. But again we must insist that they did not reach the threshold of the human world. They entered, as it were, a blind alley.

For the sake of a clear statement of the problem we must carefully distinguish between *signs* and *symbols*. That we find rather complex systems of signs and signals in animal behavior seems to be an ascertained fact. We may even say that some animals, especially domesticated animals, are expremely susceptible to signs.[14] A dog will react to the slightest changes in the behavior of his master; he will even distinguish the expressions of a human face or the modulations of a human voice.[15] But it is a far cry

[14] This susceptibility has, for instance, been proved in the famous case of "clever Hans" which a few decades ago created something of a sensation among psychobiologists. Clever Hans was a horse which appeared to possess an astounding intelligence. He could even master rather complicated arithmetical problems, extract cube roots, and so on, stamping on the ground as many times as the solution of the problem required. A special committee of psychologists and other scientists was called on to investigate the case. It soon became clear that the animal reacted to certain involuntary movements of its owner. When the owner was absent or did not understand the question, the horse could not answer it.

[15] To illustrate this point I should like to mention another revealing example. The psychobiologist, Dr. Pfungst, who had developed some new and interesting methods for the study of animal behavior, once told me that he had received a letter from a major about a curious problem. The major had a dog which accompanied him on his walks. Whenever the master got ready to go out the animal showed signs of great joy and excitement. But one day the major decided to try a little experiment. Pretending to go out, he put on his hat, took his cane, and made the customary preparations—without, however, any intention of going for a walk. To his great surprise the dog was not in the least deceived; he remained quietly in his corner. After a brief period of observation Dr. Pfungst was able to solve the mystery. In the major's room there was a desk with a drawer which contained some valuable and important documents. The major had formed the habit of rattling this drawer before leaving the house in order to make sure that it was safely locked. He did not do so the day he did not intend to go out. But for the dog this had become a signal, a necessary element of the walk-situation. Without this signal the dog did not react.

from these phenomena to an understanding of symbolic and human speech. The famous experiments of Pavlov prove only that animals can easily be trained to react not merely to direct stimuli but to all sorts of mediate or representative stimuli. A bell, for example, may become a "sign for dinner," and an animal may be trained not to touch its food when this sign is absent. But from this we learn only that the experimenter, in this case, has succeeding in changing the food-situation of the animal. He has complicated this situation by voluntarily introducing into it a new element. All the phenomena which are commonly described as conditioned reflexes are not merely very far from but even opposed to the essential character of human symbolic thought. Symbols—in the proper sense of this term—cannot be reduced to mere signals. Signals and symbols belong to two different universes of discourse: a signal is a part of the physical world of being; a symbol is a part of the human world of meaning. Signals are "operators"; symbols are "designators." [16] Signals, even when understood and used as such, have nevertheless a sort of physical or substantial being; symbols have only a functional value.

Bearing this distinction in mind, we can find an approach to one of the most controverted problems. The question of the *intelligence of animals* has always been one of the greatest puzzles of anthropological philosophy. Tremendous efforts, both of thought and observation, have been expended on answers to this question. But the ambiguity and vagueness of the very term "intelligence" has always stood in the way of a clear solution. How can we hope to answer a question whose import we do not understand? Metaphysicians and scientists, naturalists and theologians have used the word intelligence in varying and contradictory senses. Some psychologists and psychobiologists have flatly refused to speak of the intelligence of animals. In all animal behavior they saw only the play of a certain automatism. This thesis had behind it the authority of Descartes; yet it has been reasserted in modern psychology. "The animal," says E. L. Thorndike in his work on animal intelligence, "does not think one is like the other, nor does it, as is so often said, mistake one for the other. It does not think *about* it at all; it just thinks *it* . . . The idea that animals react to a particular and

[16] For the distinction between operators and designators see Charles Morris, "The Foundation of the Theory of Signs," *Encyclopedia of the Unified Sciences* (1938).

absolutely defined and realized sense-impression, and that a similar reaction to a sense-impression which varies from the first proves an association by similarity, is a myth." [17] Later and more exact observations led to a different conclusion. In the case of the higher animals it became clear that they were able to solve rather difficult problems and that these solutions were not brought about in a merely mechanical way, by trial and error. As Koehler points out, the most striking difference exists between a mere chance solution and a genuine solution, so that the one can easily be distinguished from the other. That at least some of the reactions of the higher animals are not merely a product of chance but guided by insight appears to be incontestable.[18] If by intelligence we understand either adjustment to the immediate environment or adaptive modification of environment, we must certainly ascribe to animals a comparatively highly developed intelligence. It must also be conceded that not all animal actions are governed by the presence of an immediate stimulus. The animal is capable of all sorts of detours in its reactions. It may learn not only to use implements but even to invent tools for its purposes. Hence some psychobiologists do not hesitate to speak of a creative or constructive imagination in animals.[19] But neither this intelligence nor this imagination is of the specifically human type. In short, we may say that the animal possesses a practical imagination and intelligence whereas man alone has developed a new form: a *symbolic imagination and intelligence.*

Moreover, in the mental development of the individual mind the transition from one form to the other—from a merely practical attitude to a symbolic attitude—is evident. But here this step is the final result of a slow and continuous process. By the usual methods of psychological observation it is not easy to distinguish the individual stages of this complicated process. There is, however, another way to obtain full insight into the general character and paramount importance of this transition. Nature itself has here, so to speak, made an experiment capable of throwing unexpected light upon the point in question. We have the classical cases of

[17] Edward L. Thorndike, *Animal Intelligence* (New York: Macmillan, 1911), pp. 119 ff.

[18] See Koehler, *op. cit.,* chap. vii, " 'Chance' and 'Imitation.' "

[19] See R. M. and A. W. Yerkes, *The Great Apes* (New Haven: Yale University Press, 1929), pp. 368 ff., 520 ff.

Laura Bridgman and Helen Keller, two blind deaf-mute children, who by means of special methods learned to speak. Although both cases are well known and have often been treated in psychological literature,[20] I must nevertheless remind the reader of them once more because they contain perhaps the best illustration of the general problem with which we are here concerned. Mrs. Sullivan, the teacher of Helen Keller, has recorded the exact data on which the child really began to understand the meaning and function of human language. I quote her own words: "I must write you a line this morning because something very important has happened. Helen has taken the second great step in her education. She has learned that *everything has a name, and that the manual alphabet is the key to everything she wants to know.*

". . . This morning, while she was washing, she wanted to know the name for 'water.' When she wants to know the name of anything, she points to it and pats my hand. I spelled 'w-a-t-e-r' and thought no more about it until after breakfast. . . . [Later on] we went out to the pump house, and I made Helen hold her mug under the spout while I pumped. As the cold water gushed forth, filling the mug, I spelled 'w-a-t-e-r' in Helen's free hand. The word coming so close upon the sensation of cold water rushing over her hand seemed to startle her. She dropped the mug and stood as one transfixed. A new light came into her face. She spelled 'water' several times. Then she dropped on the ground and asked for its name and pointed to the pump and the trellis and suddenly turning round she asked for my name. I spelled 'teacher.' All the way back to the house she was highly excited, and learned the name of every object she touched, so that in a few hours she had added thirty new words to her vocabulary. The next morning she got up like a radiant fairy. She has flitted from object to object, asking the name of everything and kissing me for very gladness. . . . Everything must have a name now. Wherever we go, she asks eagerly for the names of things she has not learned at home. She is anxious for her friends to spell, and eager to teach the letters to everyone she meets. She drops the signs and pantomime she

[20] For Laura Bridgman see Maud Howe and Florence Howe Hall, *Laura Bridgman* (Boston, 1903); Mary Swift Lamson, *Life and Education of Laura Dewey Bridgman* (Boston, 1881); Wilhelm Jerusalem, *Laura Bridgman. Erziehung einer Taubstumm-Blinden* (Berlin, 1905).

used before, as soon as she has words to supply their place, and the acquirement of a new word affords her the liveliest pleasure. And we notice that her face grows more expressive each day." [21]

The decisive step leading from the use of signs and pantomime to the use of words, that is, of symbols, could scarcely be described in a more striking manner. What was the child's real discovery at this moment? Helen Keller had previously learned to combine a certain thing or event with a certain sign of the manual alphabet. A fixed association had been established between these things and certain tactile impressions. But a series of such associations, even if they are repeated and amplified, still does not imply an understanding of what human speech is and means. In order to arrive at such an understanding the child had to make a new and much more significant discovery. It had to understand that *everything has a name*—that the symbolic function is not restricted to particular cases but is a principle of *universal* applicability which encompasses the whole field of human thought. In the case of Helen Keller this discovery came as a sudden shock. She was a girl of seven years of age who, with the exception of defects in the use of certain sense organs, was in an excellent state of health and possessed of a highly developed mind. By the neglect of her education she had been very much retarded. Then, suddenly, the crucial development takes place. It works like an intellectual revolution. The child begins to see the world in a new light. It has learned the use of words not merely as mechanical signs or signals but as an entirely new instrument of thought. A new horizon is opened up, and henceforth the child will roam at will in this incomparably wider and freer area.

The same can be shown in the case of Laura Bridgman, though hers is a less spectacular story. Both in mental ability and in intellectual development Laura Bridgman was greatly inferior to Helen Keller. Her life and education do not contain the same dramatic elements we find in Helen Keller. Yet in both cases the same typical elements are present. After Laura Bridgman had learned the use of the finger-alphabet she, too, suddenly reached the point at which she began to understand the symbolism of human speech. In this respect we find a surprising parallelism

[21] See Helen Keller, *The Story of My Life* (New York: Doubleday, Page and Co., 1902, 1903), Supplementary Account of Helen Keller's Life and Education, pp. 315 ff.

between the two cases. "I shall never forget," writes Miss Drew, one of the first teachers of Laura Bridgman, "the first meal taken after she appreciated the use of the finger-alphabet. Every article that she touched must have a name; and I was obliged to call some one to help me wait upon the other children, while she kept me busy in spelling the new words." [22]

The principle of symbolism, with its universality, validity, and general applicability, is the magic word, the Open Sesame! giving access to the specifically human world, to the world of human culture. Once man is in possession of this magic key further progress is assured. Such progress is evidently not obstructed or made impossible by any lack in the sense material. The case of Helen Keller, who reached a very high degree of mental development and intellectual culture, shows us clearly and irrefutably that a human being in the construction of his human world is not dependent upon the quality of his sense material. If the theories of sensationalism were right, if every idea were nothing but a faint copy of an original sense impression, then the condition of a blind, deaf, and dumb child would indeed be desperate. For it would be deprived of the very sources of human knowledge; it would be, as it were, an exile from reality. But if we study Helen Keller's autobiography we are at once aware that this is untrue, and at the same time we understand why it is untrue. Human culture derives its specific character and its intellectual and moral values, not from the material of which it consists, but from its form, its architectural structure. And this form may be expressed in any sense material. Vocal language has a very great technical advantage over tactile language; but the technical defects of the latter do not destroy its essential use. The free development of symbolic thought and symbolic expression is not obstructed by the use of tactile signs in the place of vocal ones. If the child has succeeded in grasping the meaning of human language, it does not matter in which particular material this meaning is accessible to it. As the case of Helen Keller proves, man can construct his symbolic world out of the poorest and scantiest materials. The thing of vital importance is not the individual bricks and stones but their general *function* as architectural form. In the realm of speech it is their general symbolic function which vivifies the material signs

[22] See Mary Swift Lamson, *Life and Education of Laura Dewey Bridgman, the Deaf, Dumb, and Blind Girl* (Boston: Houghton, Mifflin Co., 1881), pp. 7 f.

and "makes them speak." Without this vivifying principle the human world would indeed remain deaf and mute. With this principle, even the world of a deaf, dumb, and blind child can become incomparably broader and richer than the world of the most highly developed animal.

PART II

Some Forms of Cognition

BERTRAND RUSSELL

Knowledge of Facts and Knowledge of Laws

Bertrand Russell (1872–   ) is the well-known contemporary English philosopher, Fellow of Trinity College, Cambridge, Nobel Prize winner, and holder of many other distinguished awards and recognitions. His first book was a major contribution to the study of Leibniz. With A. N. Whitehead, Russell turned the study of logic and the philosophy of mathematics in the direction it has since taken. His list of publications is staggering. The work from which the following selection is taken constitutes the culmination of his writings in theory of knowledge.

When we examine our beliefs as to matters of fact, we find that they are sometimes based directly on perception or memory, while in other cases they are inferred. To common sense this distinction presents little difficulty: the beliefs that arise immediately from perception appear to it indubitable, and the inferences, though they may sometimes be wrong, are thought, in such cases, to be fairly easily rectified except where peculiarly dubious matters are concerned. I know of the existence of Napoleon because I have heard and read about him, and I have every reason to believe in the veracity of my teachers. I am somewhat less certain about Hengist and Horsa, and much less certain about Zoroaster, but

From Bertrand Russell, *Human Knowledge, Its Scope and Limits* (New York: Simon & Schuster, 1948), Chap. I, Part 3, pp. 165–175. Copyright, 1948, by Bertrand Russell. Reprinted by permission of Simon & Schuster, Inc. and George Allen & Unwin Ltd., London.

these uncertainties are still on a common-sense level, and do not seem, at first sight, to raise any philosophical issue.

This primitive confidence, however, was lost at a very early stage in philosophical speculation, and was lost for sound reasons. It was found that what I know by perception is less than had been thought, and that the inferences by which I pass from perceived to unperceived facts are open to question. Both these sources of skepticism must be investigated.

There is, to begin with, a difficulty as to what is inferred and what is not. I spoke a moment ago of my belief in Napoleon as an inference from what I have heard and read, but there is an important sense in which this is not quite true. When a child is being taught history, he does not argue: "My teacher is a person of the highest moral character, paid to teach me facts; my teacher says there was such a person as Napoleon; therefore probably there was such a person." If he did, he would retain considerable doubt, since his evidence of the teacher's moral character is likely to be inadequate, and in many countries at many times teachers have been paid to teach the opposite of facts. The child in fact, unless he hates the teacher, spontaneously believes what he is told. When we are told anything emphatically or authoritatively, it is an effort not to believe it, as anyone can experience on April Fools' Day. Nevertheless there is still a distinction, even on a common-sense level, between what we are told and what we know for ourselves. If you say to the child, "How do you know about Napoleon?", the child may say, "Because my teacher told me." If you say, "How do you know your teacher told you?", the child may say, "Why, of course, because I heard her." If you say, "How do you know you heard her?", he may say, "Because I remember it distinctly." If you say, "How do you know you remember it?", he will either lose his temper or say, "Well, I do remember it." Until you reach this point, he will defend his belief as to a matter of fact by belief in another matter of fact, but in the end he reaches a belief for which he can give no further reason.

There is thus a distinction between beliefs that arise spontaneously and beliefs for which no further reason can be given. It is the latter class of beliefs that are of most importance for theory of knowledge, since they are the indispensable minimum of premises for our knowledge of matters of fact. Such beliefs I shall call "data." In ordinary thinking they are *causes* of other beliefs rather than *premises* from which other beliefs are inferred; but in a critical scrutiny of our beliefs as to matters of fact we must whenever possible translate the causal transitions of primitive thinking into logical transitions, and only accept the derived beliefs to the extent that the character of the transitions seems to justify. For this there is a common-sense reason, namely, that every such transition is found to involve some risk of error, and therefore data are more nearly certain than beliefs derived from them. I am not contending that data are ever completely certain, nor is this contention necessary for their importance in theory of knowledge.

There is a long history of discussions as to what was mistakenly called "skepticism of the senses." Many appearances are deceptive. Things seen in a mirror may be thought to be "real." In certain circumstances, people see double. The rainbow seems to touch the ground at some point, but if you go there you do not find it. Most noteworthy in this connection are dreams: however vivid they may have been, we believe, when we wake up, that the objects which we thought we saw were illusory. But in all these cases the core of data is not illusory, but only the derived beliefs. My visual sensations, when I look in a mirror or see double, are exactly what I think they are. Things at the foot of the rainbow do really look colored. In dreams I have all the experiences that I seem to have; it is only things outside my mind that are not as I believe them to be while I am dreaming. There are in fact no illusions of the senses, but only mistakes in interpreting sensational data as signs of things other than themselves. Or, to speak more exactly, there is no evidence that there are illusions of the senses.

Every sensation which is of a familiar kind brings with it various associated beliefs and expectations. When, say, we see and hear an airplane, we do not merely have the visual sensation and the auditory sensation of a whirring noise; spontaneously and without conscious thought we interpret what we see and hear and fill it out with customary adjuncts. To what an extent we do this becomes obvious when we make a mistake—for example, when what we thought was an airplane turns out to be a bird. I knew a road, along which I used often to go in a car, which had a bend at a certain place, and a whitewashed wall straight ahead. At night it was very difficult not to see the wall as a road going straight on up a hill. The right interpretation as a house and the wrong interpretation as an uphill road were both, in a sense, inferences from the sensational datum, but they were not inferences in the logical sense, since they occurred without any conscious mental process.

I gave the name "animal inference" to the process of spontaneous interpretation of sensations. When a dog hears himself called in tones to which he is accustomed, he looks round and runs in the direction of the sound. He may be deceived, like the dog looking into the gramophone in the advertisement of "His Master's Voice." But since inferences of this sort are generated by the repeated experiences that give rise to habit, his inference must be one which has usually been right in his past life, since otherwise the habit would not have been generated. We thus find ourselves, when we begin to reflect, expecting all sorts of things that in fact happen, although it would be logically possible for them not to happen in spite of the occurrence of the sensations which give rise to the expectations. Thus reflection upon animal inference gives us an initial store of scientific laws, such as "Dogs bark." These initial laws are usually somewhat unreliable, but they help us to take the first steps toward science.

Everyday generalizations, such as "Dogs bark," come to be explicitly believed after habits have been generated which might be described as a pre-verbal form of the same belief. What sort of habit is it that comes to be expressed in the words "Dogs bark"? We do not expect them to bark at all times, but we do expect that *if* they make a noise it will be a bark or a growl. Psychologically, induction does not proceed as it does in the textbooks, where we are supposed to have observed a number of occasions on which dogs barked, and then proceeded consciously to generalize. The fact is that the generalization, in the form of a habit of expectation, occurs at a lower level than that of conscious thought, so that, when we begin to think consciously, we find ourselves believing the generalization, not, explicitly, on the basis of the evidence, but as expressing what is implicit in our habit of expectation. This is a history of the belief, not a justification of it.

Let us make this state of affairs somewhat more explicit. First comes the repeated experience of dogs barking, then comes the habit of expecting a bark, then, by giving verbal expression to the habit, comes belief in the general proposition "Dogs bark." Last comes the logician, who asks not "Why do I believe this?" but "What reason is there for supposing this true?" Clearly the reason, if any, must consist of two parts: first, the facts of perception consisting of the various occasions on which we have heard dogs bark; second, some principle justifying generalization from observed instances to a law. But this logical process comes historically after, not before, our belief in a host of common-sense generalizations.[1]

The translation of animal inferences into verbal generalizations is carried out very inadequately in ordinary thinking, and even in the thinking of many philosophers. In what counts as perception of external objects there is much that consists of habits generated by past experience. Take, for example, our belief in the permanence of objects. When we see a dog or a cat, a chair or a table, we do not suppose that we are seeing something which has a merely momentary existence; we are convinced that what we are seeing has a past and a future of considerable duration. We do not think this about everything that we see; a flash of lightning, a rocket, or a rainbow is expected to disappear quickly. But experience has generated in us the expectation that ordinary solid objects, which can be touched as well as seen, usually persist, and can be seen and touched again on suitable occasions. Science reinforces this belief by explaining away apparent disappearances as transformations into gaseous forms. But the belief in quasi-permanence, except in exceptional cases, antedates the scientific doctrine of the indestructibility of matter, and is itself antedated by the animal expectation that common objects can be seen again if we look in the right place.

The filling out of the sensational core by means of animal inferences, until it becomes what is called "perception," is analogous to the filling out of telegraphic press messages in newspaper offices. The reporter telegraphs the one word "King," and the newspaper prints "His Gracious Majesty King George VI." There is some risk of error in this proceeding, since the reporter may have been relating the doings of Mr. Mackenzie King. It is true that the context would usually reveal such an error, but one can imagine circumstances in which it would not. In dreams, we fill out the bare sensational message wrongly, and only the context of waking life shows us our mistake.

The analogy to abbreviated press telegrams is very close. Sup-

---

[1] The reader should relate this paragraph to selection 6—Hume, "Knowledge and Induction"—in this anthology.—Ed.

pose, for instance, you see a friend at the window of an incoming train, and a little later you see him coming toward you on the platform. The physical causes of your perceptions (and of your interpretation of them) are certain light signals passing between him and your eyes. All that physics, by itself, entitles you to infer from the receipt of these signals is that, somewhere along the line of sight, light of the appropriate colors has been emitted or reflected or refracted or scattered. It is obvious that the kind of ingenuity which has produced the cinema could cause you to have just these sensations in the absence of your friend, and that in that case you would be deceived. But such sources of deception cannot be frequent, or at least cannot have been frequent hitherto, since, if they were, you would not have formed the habits of expectation and belief in context that you have in fact formed. In the case supposed, you are confident that it is your friend, that he has existed throughout the interval between seeing him at the window and seeing him on the platform, and that he has pursued a continuous path through space from the one to the other. You have no doubt that what you saw was something solid, not an intangible object like a rainbow or a cloud. And so, although the message received by the senses contains (so to speak) only a few key words, your mental and physical habits cause you, spontaneously and without thought, to expand it into a coherent and amply informative dispatch.

This expansion of the sensational core to produce what goes by the somewhat question-begging name of "perception" is obviously only trustworthy in so far as our habits of association run parallel to processes in the external world. Clouds looked down upon from a mountain may look so like the sea or a field of snow that only positive knowledge to the contrary prevents you from so interpreting your visual sensations. If you are not accustomed to the gramophone, you will confidently believe that the voice you hear on the other side of the door proceeds from a person in the room that you are about to enter. There is no obvious limit to the invention of ingenious apparatus capable of deceiving the unwary. We know that the people we see on the screen in the cinema are not really there, although they move and talk and behave in a manner having some resemblance to that of human beings; but if we did not know it, we might at first find it hard to believe. Thus what we seem to know through the senses may be deceptive whenever the environment is different from what our past experience has led us to expect.

From the above considerations it follows that we cannot admit as data all that an uncritical acceptance of common sense would take as given in perception. Only sensations and memories are truly data for our knowledge of the external world. We must exclude from our list of data not only the things that we consciously infer, but all that is obtained by animal inference, such as the imagined hardness of an object seen but not touched. It is true that our "perceptions," in all their fullness, are data for psychology: we do in fact have the experience of believing in such-and-such an object. It is only for knowledge of things outside our own minds that it is necessary to regard only sensations as data. This necessity is a consequence of what we know of physics and physiology. The same external stimulus, reaching the brains of two men with different experiences, will produce different results, and it is only what these different results have in common that can be used in inferring external causes. If it is objected that the truth of physics and physiology is doubtful, the situation is even worse; for if they are false, nothing whatever as to the outer world can be inferred from my experiences. I am, however, throughout this work, assuming that science is broadly speaking true.

If we define "data" as "those matters of fact of which, independently of inference, we have a right to feel most nearly certain," it follows from what has been said that all my data are events that happen to me, and are, in fact, what would commonly be called events in my mind. This is a view which has been characteristic of British empiricism,[2] but has been rejected by most Continental philosophers, and is not now accepted by the followers of Dewey or by most of the logical positivists. As the issue is of considerable importance, I shall set forth the reasons which have convinced me, including a brief repetition of those that have already been given.

There are, first, arguments on the common-sense level, derived from illusions, squinting, reflection, refraction, etc., but above all from dreams. I dreamed last night that I was in Germany, in a house which looked out on a ruined church; in my dream I sup-

[2] Locke is one of the best examples of a British empiricist. The readings from Locke included in this anthology can be taken as representative of empiricism.—Ed.

posed at first that the church had been bombed during the recent
war, but was subsequently informed that its destruction dated from
the wars of religion in the sixteenth century. All this, so long as I
remained asleep, had all the convincingness of waking life. I did
really have the dream, and did really have an experience in-
trinsically indistinguishable from that of seeing a ruined church
when awake. It follows that the experience which I call "seeing
a church" is not conclusive evidence that there is a church, since
it may occur when there is no such external object as I suppose
in my dream. It may be said that, though when dreaming I may
think that I am awake, when I wake up I *know* that I am awake.
But I do not see how we are to have any such certainty; I have
frequently dreamed that I woke up; in fact once, after ether, I
dreamed it about a hundred times in the course of one dream.
We condemn dreams, in fact, because they do not fit into a proper
context, but this argument can be made inconclusive, as in
Calderon's play *La Vida es Sueño*. I do not believe that I am now
dreaming, but I cannot prove that I am not. I am, however, quite
certain that I am having certain experiences, whether they be those
of a dream or those of waking life.[3]

We come now to another class of arguments, derived from physics
and physiology. This class of arguments came into philosophy with
Locke, who used it to show that secondary qualities are subjective.[4]
This class of arguments is capable of being used to throw doubt
on the truth of the physics and physiology, but I will first deal with
them on the hypothesis that science, in the main, is true.

We experience a visual sensation when light waves reach the
eye, and an auditory sensation when sound waves reach the ear.
There is no reason to suppose that light waves are at all like the experience which we call seeing something, or sound waves at all like
the experience which we call hearing a sound. There is no reason
whatever to suppose that the physical sources of light and sound
waves have any more resemblance to our experiences than the
waves have. If the waves are produced in unusual ways, our ex-

[3] The argument in this paragraph finds its prototype in Descartes. Cf.
selection 9 in this anthology.—Ed.
[4] Secondary qualities are those like color, sound, taste, and smell. They
have traditionally been distinguished from 'primary qualities' like shape, size,
extension, motion, which have been said to be 'objective,' that is, to exist independent of perception.—Ed.

perience may lead us to infer subsequent experiences which it turns out that we do not have; this shows that even in normal perception interpretation plays a larger part than common sense supposes, and that interpretation sometimes leads us to entertain false expectations.

Another difficulty is connected with time. We see and hear now, but what (according to common sense) we are seeing and hearing occurred some time ago. When we both see and hear an explosion, we see it first and hear it afterward. Even if we could suppose that the furniture of our room is exactly what it seems, we cannot suppose this of a nebula millions of light-years away, which looks like a speck but is not much smaller than the Milky Way, and of which the light that reaches us now started before human beings began to exist. And the difference between the nebula and the furniture is only one of degree.

Then there are physiological arguments. People who have lost a leg may continue to feel pain in it. Dr. Johnson, disproving Berkeley, thought the pain in his toe when he kicked a stone was evidence for the existence of the stone, but it appears that it was not even evidence for the existence of his toe, since he might have felt it even if his toe had been amputated. Speaking generally, if a nerve is stimulated in a given manner, a certain sensation results, whatever may be the source of the stimulation. Given sufficient skill, it ought to be possible to make a man see the starry heavens by tickling his optic nerve, but the instrument used would bear little resemblance to the august bodies studied by astronomers.

The above arguments, as I remarked before, may be interpreted skeptically, as showing that there is no reason to believe that our sensations have external causes. As this interpretation concedes what I am at present engaged in maintaining—namely, that sensations are the sole data for physics—I shall not, for the moment, consider whether it can be refuted, but shall pass on to a closely similar line of argument which is related to the method of Cartesian doubt. This method consists in searching for data by provisionally rejecting everything that it is found possible to call in question.

Descartes argues that the existence of sensible objects might be uncertain, because it would be possible for a deceitful demon to mislead us. *We* should substitute for a deceitful demon a cinema in technicolor. It is, of course, also possible that we may be dreaming. But he regards the existence of our thoughts as wholly unquestionable. When he says, "I think, therefore I am," the primitive certainties at which he may be supposed to have arrived are particular "thoughts," in the large sense in which he uses the term. His own existence is an inference from his thoughts, an inference whose validity does not at the moment concern us. In the context, what appears certain to him is that there is doubting, but the experience of doubting has no special prerogative over other experiences. When I see a flash of lightning I may, it is maintained, be uncertain as to the physical character of lightning and even as to whether anything external to myself has happened, but I cannot make myself doubt that there has been the occurrence which is called "seeing a flash of lightning," though there may have been no flash outside my seeing.

It is not suggested that I am certain about all my own experiences; this would certainly be false. Many memories are dubious, and so are many faint sensations. What I am saying—and in this I am expounding part of Descartes's argument—is that there are some occurrences that I cannot make myself doubt, and that these are all of the kind that, if we admit a not-self, are part of the life of myself. Not all of them are sensations; some are abstract thoughts, some are memories, some are wishes, some are pleasures or pains. But all are what we should commonly describe as mental events in me.

My own view is that this point of view is in the right in so far as it is concerned with data that are matters of fact. Matters of fact that lie outside my experience can be made to seem doubtful, unless there is an argument showing that their existence follows from matters of fact within my experience together with laws of whose certainty I feel reasonably convinced. But this is a long question, concerning which, at the moment, I wish to say only a few preliminary words.

Hume's skepticism [5] with regard to the world of science resulted from (a) the doctrine that all my data are private to me, together with (b) the discovery that matters of fact, however numerous and well selected, never logically imply any other matter of fact. I do not see any way of escaping from either of these theses. The first I have been arguing; I may say that I attach especial weight in this respect to the argument from the physical causation of sensations. As to the second, it is obvious as a matter of syntax to

[5] The selections from Hume included in this anthology elaborate his scepticism, as well as the two doctrines here referred to.—Ed.

anyone who has grasped the nature of deductive arguments. A matter of fact which is not contained in the premises must require for its assertion a proper name which does not occur in the premises. But there is only one way in which a new proper name can occur in a deductive argument, and that is when we proceed from the general to the particular, as in "All men are mortal, therefore Socrates is mortal." Now, no collection of assertions of matters of fact is logically equivalent to a general assertion, so that, if our premises concern only matters of fact, this way of introducing a new proper name is not open to us. Hence the thesis follows.

If we are not to deduce Hume's skepticism from the above two premises,[6] there seems to be only one possible way of escape, and that is to maintain that among the premises of our knowledge, there are some general propositions, or there is at least one general proposition, which is not analytically necessary, i.e., the hypothesis of its falsehood is not self-contradictory. A principle justifying the scientific use of induction would have this character. What is needed is some way of giving probability (not certainty) to the inferences from known matters of fact to occurrences which have not yet been, and perhaps never will be, part of the experience of the person making the inference. If an individual is to know anything beyond his own experiences up to the present moment, his stock of uninferred knowledge must consist not only of matters of fact but also of general laws, or at least a law, allowing him to make inferences from matters of fact; and such law or laws must, unlike the principles of deductive logic, be synthetic, i.e., not proved true by their falsehood being self-contradictory. The only alternative to this hypothesis is complete skepticism as to all the inferences of science and common sense, including those which I have called animal inferences.

[6] Hume's own statement of his scepticism is given in the final selection of this anthology.—Ed.

Memory-Knowledge

H. H. Price (1899–   ), contemporary English philosopher, Wykeham Professor of Logic, New College, Oxford, Gifford lecturer, has published primarily on theory of knowledge and the history of philosophy. His two most important books are both in theory of knowledge: Perception *(London: Methuen, 1932) and* Thinking and Experience *(London: Hutchinson, 1953).*

In this paper I wish to discuss two main topics. First, I wish to offer some arguments in support of the distinction which some philosophers have drawn between memory-knowledge and memory-belief. Secondly, assuming the distinction to be accepted I wish to discuss certain questions which consequently arise with regard to the nature of memory-images.

It is held by those who make this distinction that we sometimes (not very often perhaps) directly apprehend or know the past, but at other times we only have beliefs about it. Knowledge of the past, as of anything else, is of course infallible, *ex vi termini*. But belief, however reasonable and however well supported by evidence, is always fallible. And it would be maintained that the failure to distinguish between them has resulted in endless confusion both in psychological and in philosophical accounts of memory. This is the distinction which I wish to consider.

In support of the distinction it may be urged that any argument designed to prove that all memory is fallible must assume that *some* memory is *in*fallible. Suppose we argue, as Descartes did in his doubting mood, that my memory has often deceived me, and that therefore all my memory-cognitions are fallible; i.e., that all memory-cognitions are beliefs (true or false) and none of them are knowings. Obviously there is a difficulty about the premise of this argument. For it is itself a proposition about the past. The evidence for it, if there is any, can only come from memory. I remember a

From H. H. Price, "Memory-Knowledge," *Proceedings of the Aristotelian Society*, Suppl. Vol. **XV** (1936), pp. 16–24. Reprinted by courtesy of the Editor of the Aristotelian Society. [The selection included in this anthology comprises part of a lead essay in a symposium read at the Joint Session of the Aristotelian Society, the Mind Association, and the Scots Philosophical Club at St. Andrews, Scotland, July 3, 1936.]

number of past rememberings, and I remember that many of them were mistaken. But if all memory is fallible, what right have I to assert that those past rememberings of mine occurred at all, or, that (if they did) they were mistaken? It may be said that I have evidence that they occurred and were mistaken, though I cannot know this. But this will not do. For the evidence has got to be evidence about the past, and where am I to get this except from other memories? If all memory is fallible, the evidence will be just as suspect as the propositions which it is supposed to support. Further, I am not entitled to assert that a past memory-act *m was mistaken,* unless I now know not merely that *m* occurred, but also that there was a certain previous state of affairs *s* which *m* mis-reported or failed to correspond with. Thus in order to assert that my memory has deceived me even once, I have to know a number of facts about the past. Unless some memory is knowledge, I have no ground for asserting that some memory is only belief. And I could not possibly have *any* ground for asserting that all memory whatever is only belief, or that all memory whatever is fallible.

In order to bring out the full force of this argument, let us take the following example. Suppose I remember spending the whole of last Wednesday in London, and on consideration I become convinced that this memory-judgment of mine is mistaken. What sort of evidence would convince me? It might be the evidence of testimony; Smith might tell me that he had tea with me last Wednesday in Oxford, and Jones might tell me that he heard me give a lecture in Oxford that morning. Or it might be the evidence of documents; I might find a pound-note in my pocket, whereas if I had gone to London I should certainly have spent it. Now none of these kinds of evidence is independent of memory. Why should not Smith and Jones be lying? What ground have I for trusting their statements? My ground is that they are reliable men. But what is my evidence for that? It is that I *remember* that I have been able to verify many of the statements which they made to me on previous occasions; or (more remotely) I *remember* that I have been able to verify statements made by other men who resembled them in face, or manner, or social status. Much the same is true of the evidence of documents. When I use the evidence of my diary, the grounds which make it reasonable for me to do so are very complicated, and presuppose the validity of memory several times over. First I must assume that when I write things in my diary, I usually believe them at the time. This is by no means a self-evident proposition. A Diarist can very well be mendacious, even if he is myself. I must therefore either *remember* that on other occasions I have usually believed what I was writing down, and so conclude by analogy that I probably believed it on that occasion; or else I must just remember directly that I did believe it on that occasion. Also I must assume that I usually record events in my diary very soon after they have happened, and further that my beliefs about the recent past are usually true. If I have any evidence for these assumptions, it can only come from memory. Lastly, I have to assume that ink-marks retain a more or less constant shape for long periods of time. If the words written in my diary were to change their shape over-night, my documentary evidence would not be worth much. And why should they not? This proposition about ink-marks is not self-evident (though some who philosophize about history seem to think that it is). It is nothing but an inductive generalization. And the evidence for this induction can only come from memory. I remember that I have often looked at written words at a date t_1, and then have looked at them again at a date t_2, a day or month or ten years later; and I remember that they did not change their shape appreciably during the interval. Similar considerations apply to all use of documents, whether their author be myself or somebody else, whether they are recorded in ink or on stone or bronze, or in any other way. In so far as the use of them is reasonable, it derives its reasonableness from induction and analogy; and the premises of the induction or analogy are provided by memory and nothing else. And this applies to the documents which psychologists compose in the course of their experiments on memory as much as to any other documents. To reach their conclusions (which are often sceptical enough) they have to trust their records. But if all memory without exception is fallible—and some of them might claim that their experiments proved this—then they have no ground for trusting any record, whether their own or anybody else's.

It is the same with the use of other physical signs. When we use them (as we often do) to verify or refute our own memory-judgments or somebody else's, we are really using memory over again; or rather, our procedure is only rational if we use memory over again. The proximate premise is an inductive generalization, and the ultimate premises are certain particular facts about the past, from which the generalization derives whatever probability it has—facts which are only accessible by means of memory. In the case of the pound note, the generalization is about my own monetary habits, but it is none the less inductive for that. It is not self-evident to me that I have such and such a character or such and such a habit (though again some writers seem to think it is). I have to *learn* about my habits, as about other people's, by induction and analogy; and the premises of my induction are, that I remember doing so and so, or feeling thus and thus, on such and such past occasions. Or again, consider this case. You say you remember waking up and hearing heavy rain at 5 a.m. this morning. How do I verify or refute this? I go out and see whether the grass is wet and the road muddy. But this would be an entirely irrelevant proceeding unless I had grounds for believing the generalization that whenever it rains heavily the grass is wet and the road muddy for several hours afterwards; and my grounds are entirely derived from memory.

These considerations—if I may digress for a moment—have some bearing on the modern theory that all empirical judgments, including memory-judgments, are really judgments about the future. For if they were not (it is asked) how could they possibly be verified? And if they could not be verified, it is held that they would not be judgments at all, and the sentences in which we profess to be uttering them would be just nonsensical concatenations of noises. Now there seems to be a lacuna in this theory, at least so far as it concerns memory-judgments. Let there be a memory-judgment *p*. How am I to know *just what* future situation will verify or refute this judgment? Only by asking myself what future consequences will follow or probably follow if the judgment be true. But how am I to know just what consequences there ought to be? I cannot see how I can possibly know what they ought to be, or have any ground for a reasonable belief about it, unless I have some *generalization* to go upon, of the form 'if *p*, then *q*', or 'if *p*, then probably *q*'. And this will always have to be an induction, the premises of which are themselves provided by other memory-judgments. If those memory-judgments are themselves predictions (as the theory maintains), we have the same difficulty over again. To verify them—and if we did not verify them we should have no business to use them as premises—we shall need still other inductive generalizations, about whose justification the same difficulty would arise afresh. To escape this, we shall have to maintain that some at least of our memory-judgments do *not* have to be verified by future events and are in no sense predictions. Some at least among them will have to be direct apprehensions of the past; so that they need no verification, and can themselves be used for the verifying or refuting of other judgments, i.e., of those which are not apprehendings, but only beliefs or opinions or takings-for-granted.

There are three other criteria which we commonly use for testing the memory-judgments of ourselves and others: namely, *recency, vividness,* and *consistency.* It should now be clear that the first two (like the criterion of future consequences) are not ultimate, but presuppose the validity of other memory-judgments. First we will consider recency. We do think that a memory-statement about a recent event is in general more likely to be true than a memory-statement about a remote one. The criterion is a pretty shaky one but we do use it with considerable confidence with regard to reports of events which happened (say) less than 24 hours ago. But the difficulty about it is glaringly obvious. A recent memory is to be trusted more than a remote one. But how do I know that such and such a memory *is* a recent one? A recent memory is one which occurs shortly after the event. But what is 'the event'? Obviously not any event you please, but a certain specific event to which (and to nothing else) this memory-act somehow refers, or which it is about. I must know that this event did in fact occur; otherwise I cannot possibly know whether the memory which I am testing is a recent one or not. Also of course I have got to know that the interval between that event and this memory about it was of such and such a length and no more. If I am to apply the test of recency to a memory of someone else's, or indeed of my own, I must have direct access to the past. Otherwise I have not the faintest prospect of discovering what is recent and what is not.

This difficulty concerns the application of the criterion. But there is also a difficulty about establishing the criterion at all. The proposition 'memories of recent events are likely to be correct' is obviously inductive, and the premises of the induction, such as they are, must themselves be *remembered* correlations. We must have memory-*knowledge* that on a number of occasions in which the interval between a memory-*belief* and its object has been short, the belief has been true more often than not.

It is obvious that the criterion of vividness is also established inductively. The generalization is that when there is a vivid memory-image, there is usually a past event corresponding to it. If it is reasonable to attach any probability at all to this generalization, I must be able to remember a number of past memory-images (some vivid and some not) and a number of past events which preceded them; and I must also be able to remember that the vivid images corresponded to the preceding events more frequently and more accurately than the faint ones did.

We must now consider the criterion of consistency. Surely there can be nothing inductive about that? And if there is not, we can use it to test our memory-judgments without having to presuppose the validity of other memory-judgments in the process. We shall have to presuppose nothing but the laws of Logic, which are either self-evident or analytic. But it appears to me that when we say we are applying the criterion of consistency to our memory-judgments or other people's, we are not usually thinking of logical consistency at all, but only of *causal* consistency, if the phrase may be allowed. If I remember being in London at 4:15 on Wednesday, and you remember seeing me in Oxford at 4:17 on that day, we should commonly say that these two memory-judgments were inconsistent. But there is no *logical* inconsistency between them whatever. The compound statement 'H. P. was in London at 4:15 and in Oxford two minutes later' is not a self-contradiction. What it states is not logically impossible. It is only at the most causally impossible. And who knows whether it is even that? There may be some day a flying-machine which will cover 54 miles in two minutes. Of course this compound statement is exceedingly improbable. We have the strongest grounds for believing it to be false, and consequently for believing that one and only one of its two constituted statements is true. But the grounds, strong though they are, are only inductive: they consist of certain physical and physiological laws which are neither self-evident nor deducible from self-evident premises; they derive their probability (for it is no more than probability) from certain observations and experiments. And these observations and experiments are all in the past. At least it is only past ones which make it reasonable for us who are not physicists to believe in these laws. For we are not now engaged in observations and experiments such as would validate them; and even if we were, it would take us a very long time, so that we should have to remember our earlier observations and experiments while we were doing our late ones.

But suppose I remember being in London at 4:15 and you remember seeing me in Oxford at the very same moment? Is not this a logical inconsistency? Not if by 'I' and 'me' you mean a certain mind or self. So far as I can see (though I expect that some authorities would disagree with me) it is not *logically* impossible for a mind to be in two places at once, in so far as a mind can be said to be in a place at all. The suggestion that the same mind could simultaneously animate two organisms, one in London and another in Oxford does not seem to me self-contradictory. It may be very improbable, but if so its improbability is, I think, only inductive. But what if by 'I' you mean only a certain body? On the ordinary definition of 'body' it is I think self-contradictory to say that the same body is in two places at once; for the proposition that a body must be in one place at one time is then analytic. But if analytic, it is also trivial. For it remains logically possible that there might be the most intimate correlation between a group of sense-data in Piccadilly Circus and another group of sense-data existing at that moment in Oxford, a correlation such that any alteration in the one group was always accompanied by a corresponding alteration in the other. This may be as improbable as you please, but it involves no self-contradiction whatever. And if there were such a correlation it would be proper to say that the two groups of sense-data were manifestations of a single *something*, which would accordingly be present in two places at once; though it would not be proper to call that something a single body. When one person says that he saw a body A in Oxford and another that he saw it in London at the same moment, it may be that they are both misdescribing a situation of this queer kind. And if they are, their judgments are logically consistent with each other, though formulated in unsuitable words. We could not say that the truth of either logically entailed the falsity of the other, and the falsity of either the truth of the other. We should indeed have strong inductive grounds for saying that the truth of either would greatly reduce the probability of the other. But here again our inductive grounds would rest ultimately upon other memory-judgments.

The position which we have now arrived at is this. There cannot be reasonable grounds for asserting or even for suspending the falsity of any memory-judgment unless the infallibility of *some* memory-judgments is assumed. And we likewise assume the infallibility of some when we use various every-day criteria for establishing, or at least making probable, the truth of those which are initially doubtful; such criteria as vividness, or recency, or the occurrence of verificatory consequences. And this is a way of stating that some memory is knowledge in the strict sense, i.e., that it is a direct or immediate apprehension of past events or situations. Of course we must also admit, and indeed maintain, that much memory is only belief. And the beliefs might have various degrees of adequacy or reasonableness, according as the evidence for them is great or small. Some perhaps are very low-grade beliefs, having hardly any evidence at all. And some perhaps are merely non-rational takings-for-granted, where the taker has strictly speaking no evidence for the proposition which he accepts, but just adopts it without question as soon as it occurs to him (though of course the proposition may happen to be true none the less). I think there is even a stage below this, where we merely contemplate a familiar-feeling image and behave as if we were taking for granted, although there is no proposition before our minds at all. This might be called 'quasi-memory' . . . and we may suspect that this is the highest that non-human animals attain to. Finally there is the stage where we merely behave as if we remembered, without having even an image before our mind, still less a proposition. This might be called 'memory in the Behaviouristic sense'. It is perfectly compatible with the utterance of long and complicated concatenations of noises, and with the production of large masses of handwriting, as for instance in an examination.

DAVID HUME

Knowledge and Induction

David Hume (1711–1776) was a Scottish philosopher who had a great influence upon modern philosophy. He published books in philosophy of religion, ethics, and theory of knowledge. Besides the book from which all the Hume selections in this anthology are taken, Hume's major writings are his Treatise of Human Nature, Enquiry Concerning the Principles of Morals, *and his* Dialogues Concerning Natural Religion.

I

When it is asked, *What is the nature of all our reasonings concerning matter of fact?* the proper answer seems to be, that they are founded on the relation of cause and effect. When again it is asked, *What is the foundation of all our reasonings and conclusions concerning that relation?* it may be replied in one word, Experience. But if we still carry on our sifting humour, and ask, *What is the foundation of all conclusions from experience?* this implies a new question, which may be of more difficult solution and explication. Philosophers, that give themselves airs of superior wisdom and sufficiency, have a hard task when they encounter persons of inquisitive dispositions, who push them from every corner to which they retreat, and who are sure at last to bring them to some dangerous dilemma. The best expedient to prevent this confusion, is to be modest in our pretensions; and even to discover the difficulty ourselves before it is objected to us. By this means, we may make a kind of merit of our very ignorance.

I shall content myself, in this section, with an easy task, and shall pretend only to give a negative answer to the question here proposed. I say then, that, even after we have experience of the operations of cause and effect, our conclusions from that experience are *not* founded on reasoning, or any process of the understanding. This answer we must endeavour both to explain and to defend.

It must certainly be allowed, that nature has kept us at a great

From David Hume, *An Enquiry Concerning Human Understanding*, ed. L. A. Selby-Bigge (Oxford: Clarendon Press, 1902). Section I is taken from Sec. IV, Part II, pp. 32–38; Section II is taken from Sec. V, Part I, pp. 40–47.

distance from all her secrets, and has afforded us only the knowledge of a few superficial qualities of objects; while she conceals from
us those powers and principles on which the influence of those objects entirely depends. Our senses inform us of the colour, weight,
and consistence of bread; but neither sense nor reason can ever inform us of those qualities which fit it for the nourishment and support of a human body. Sight or feeling conveys an idea of the actual
motion of bodies; but as to that wonderful force or power, which
would carry on a moving body for ever in a continued change of
place, and which bodies never lose but by communicating it to
others; of this we cannot form the most distant conception. But
notwithstanding this ignorance of natural powers [1] and principles,
we always presume, when we see like sensible qualities, that they
have like secret powers, and expect that effects, similar to those
which we have experienced, will follow from them. If a body of like
colour and consistence with that bread, which we have formerly eat,
be presented to us, we make no scruple of repeating the experiment,
and foresee, with certainty, like nourishment and support. Now this
is a process of the mind or thought, of which I would willingly
know the foundation. It is allowed on all hands that there is no
known connexion between the sensible qualities and the secret
powers; and consequently, that the mind is not led to form such a
conclusion concerning their constant and regular conjunction, by
anything which it knows of their nature. As to past *Experience*,
it can be allowed to give *direct* and *certain* information of those
precise objects only, and that precise period of time, which fell
under its cognizance: but why this experience should be extended
to future times, and to other objects, which for aught we know,
may be only in appearance similar; this is the main question on
which I would insist. The bread, which I formerly eat, nourished
me; that is, a body of such sensible qualities was, at that time,
endued with such secret powers: but does it follow, that other bread
must also nourish me at another time, and that like sensible qualities
must always be attended with like secret powers? The consequence
seems nowise necessary. At least, it must be acknowledged that
there is here a consequence drawn by the mind; that there is a
certain step taken; a process of thought, and an inference, which

[1] The word *power* is here used in a loose and popular sense. The more
accurate explication of it would give additional evidence to this argument. See
Sec. 7 [of the *Enquiry*].

wants to be explained. These two propositions are far from being the same, *I have found that such an object has always been attended with such an effect,* and *I foresee, that other objects, which are, in appearance, similar, will be attended with similar effects.* I shall allow, if you please, that the one proposition may justly be inferred from the other: I know, in fact, that it always is inferred. But if you insist that the inference is made by a chain of reasoning, I desire you to produce that reasoning. The connexion between these propositions is not intuitive. There is required a medium, which may enable the mind to draw such an inference, if indeed it be drawn by reasoning and argument. What that medium is, I must confess, passes my comprehension; and it is incumbent on those to produce it, who assert that it really exists, and is the origin of all our conclusions concerning matter of fact.

This negative argument must certainly, in process of time, become altogether convincing, if many penetrating and able philosophers shall turn their enquiries this way and no one be ever able to discover any connecting proposition or intermediate step, which supports the understanding in this conclusion. But as the question is yet new, every reader may not trust so far to his own penetration, as to conclude, because an argument escapes his enquiry, that therefore it does not really exist. For this reason it may be requisite to venture upon a more difficult task; and enumerating all the branches of human knowledge, endeavour to show that none of them can afford such an argument.

All reasonings may be divided into two kinds, namely, demonstrative reasoning, or that concerning relations of ideas,[2] and moral reasoning, or that concerning matter of fact and existence. That there are no demonstrative arguments in the case seems evident; since it implies no contradiction that the course of nature may change, and that an object, seemingly like those which we have experienced, may be attended with different or contrary effects. May I not clearly and distinctly conceive that a body, falling from the clouds, and which, in all other respects, resembles snow, has yet the taste of salt or feeling of fire? Is there any more intelligible proposition than to affirm, that all the trees will flourish in December and

---

[2] Hume's phrase, "relations of ideas," marks a contrast with "matter of fact." It is best thought of as referring to reasoning like that found in geometry, where terms are defined, axioms specified, and conclusions drawn on the basis of premises employing these terms and axioms.—Ed.

January, and decay in May and June? Now whatever is intelligible, and can be distinctly conceived, implies no contradiction, and can never be proved false by any demonstrative argument or abstract reasoning *à priori*.

If we be, therefore, engaged by arguments to put trust in past experience, and make it the standard of our future judgement, these arguments must be probable only, or such as regard matter of fact and real existence, according to the division above mentioned. But that there is no argument of this kind, must appear, if our explication of that species of reasoning be admitted as solid and satisfactory. We have said that all arguments concerning existence are founded on the relation of cause and effect; that our knowledge of that relation is derived entirely from experience; and that all our experimental conclusions proceed upon the supposition that the future will be conformable to the past. To endeavour, therefore, the proof of this last supposition by probable arguments, or arguments regarding existence, must be evidently going in a circle, and taking that for granted, which is the very point in question.

In reality, all arguments from experience are founded on the similarity which we discover among natural objects, and by which we are induced to expect effects similar to those which we have found to follow from such objects. And though none but a fool or madman will ever pretend to dispute the authority of experience, or to reject that great guide of human life, it may surely be allowed a philosopher to have so much curiosity at least as to examine the principle of human nature, which gives this mighty authority to experience, and makes us draw advantage from that similarity which nature has placed among different objects. From causes which appear *similar* we expect similar effects. This is the sum of all our experimental conclusions. Now it seems evident that, if this conclusion were formed by reason, it would be as perfect at first, and upon one instance, as after ever so long a course of experience. But the case is far otherwise. Nothing so like as eggs; yet no one, on account of this appearing similarity, expects the same taste and relish in all of them. It is only after a long course of uniform experiments in any kind, that we attain a firm reliance and security with regard to a particular event. Now where is that process of reasoning which, from one instance, draws a conclusion, so different from that which it infers from a hundred instances that are nowise different from that single one? This question I propose as much for the sake of information, as with an intention of raising difficulties. I cannot find, I cannot imagine any such reasoning. But I keep my mind still open to instruction, if any one will vouchsafe to bestow it on me.

Should it be said that, from a number of uniform experiments, we *infer* a connexion between the sensible qualities and the secret powers; this, I must confess, seems the same difficulty, couched in different terms. The question still recurs, on what process of argument this *inference* is founded? Where is the medium, the interposing ideas, which join propositions so very wide of each other? It is confessed that the colour, consistence, and other sensible qualities of bread appear not, of themselves, to have any connexion with the secret powers of nourishment and support. For otherwise we could infer these secret powers from the first appearance of these sensible qualities, without the aid of experience; contrary to the sentiment of all philosophers, and contrary to plain matter of fact. Here, then, is our natural state of ignorance with regard to the powers and influence of all objects. How is this remedied by experience? It only shows us a number of uniform effects, resulting from certain objects, and teaches us that those particular objects, at that particular time, were endowed with such powers and forces. When a new object, endowed with similar sensible qualities, is produced, we expect similar powers and forces, and look for a like effect. From a body of like colour and consistence with bread we expect like nourishment and support. But this surely is a step or progress of the mind, which wants to be explained. When a man says, *I have found, in all past instances, such sensible qualities conjoined with such secret powers:* And when he says, *Similar sensible qualities will always be conjoined with similar secret powers,* he is not guilty of a tautology, nor are these propositions in any respect the same. You say that the one proposition is an inference from the other. But you must confess that the inference is not intuitive; neither is it demonstrative: Of what nature is it, then? To say it is experimental, is begging the question. For all inferences from experience suppose, as their foundation, that the future will resemble the past, and that similar powers will be conjoined with similar sensible qualities. If there be any suspicion that the course of nature may change, and that the past may be no rule for the future, all experience becomes useless, and can give rise to no inference or conclusion. It is impossible, therefore, that any arguments from experience can prove this resemblance of the past to the future; since all these arguments are founded on the supposition of that resemblance. Let the course of things be allowed hitherto ever so regular; that alone, without some new argument or inference, proves not that, for the future, it will continue so. In vain do you pretend to have learned the nature of bodies from your past experience. Their secret nature, and consequently all their effects and influence, may change, without any change in their sensible qualities. This happens sometimes, and with regard to some objects: Why may it not happen always, and with regard to all objects? What logic, what process of argument secures you against this supposition? My practice, you say, refutes my doubts. But you mistake the purport of my question. As an agent, I am quite satisfied in the point; but as a philosopher, who has some share of curiosity, I will not say scepticism, I want to learn the foundation of this inference. No reading, no enquiry has yet been able to remove my difficulty, or give me satisfaction in a matter of such importance. Can I do better than propose the difficulty to the public, even though, perhaps, I have small hopes of obtaining a solution? We shall at least, by this means, be sensible of our ignorance, if we do not augment our knowledge.

II

The passion for philosophy, like that for religion, seems liable to this inconvenience, that, though it aims at the correction of our manners, and extirpation of our vices, it may only serve, by imprudent management, to foster a predominant inclination, and push the mind, with more determined resolution, towards that side which already *draws* too much, by the bias and propensity of the natural temper. It is certain that, while we aspire to the magnanimous firmness of the philosophic sage, and endeavour to confine our pleasures altogether within our own minds, we may, at last, render our philosophy like that of Epictetus, and other *Stoics*, only a more refined system of selfishness, and reason ourselves out of all virtue as well as social enjoyment. While we study with attention the vanity of human life, and turn all our thoughts towards the empty and transitory nature of riches and honours, we are, perhaps, all the while flattering our natural indolence, which, hating the hustle of the world, and drudgery of business, seeks a pretence of reason to give itself a full and uncontrolled indulgence. There is, however, one species of philosophy which seems little liable to this inconvenience, and that because it strikes in with no disorderly passion of the human mind, nor can mingle itself with any natural affection or propensity; and that is the Academic or Sceptical philosophy. The academics always talk of doubt and suspense of judgment, of danger in hasty determinations, of confining to very narrow bounds the enquiries of the understanding, and of renouncing all speculations which lie not within the limits of common life and practice. Nothing, therefore, can be more contrary than such a philosophy to the supine indolence of the mind, its rash arrogance, its lofty pretensions, and its superstitious credulity. Every passion is mortified by it, except the love of truth; and that passion never is, nor can be, carried to too high a degree. It is surprising, therefore, that this philosophy, which, in almost every instance, must be harmless and innocent, should be the subject of so much groundless reproach and obloquy. But, perhaps, the very circumstance which renders it so innocent is what chiefly exposes it to the public hatred and resentment. By flattering no irregular passion, it gains few partizans: By opposing so many vices and follies, it raises to itself abundance of enemies, who stigmatize it as libertine, profane, and irreligious.

Nor need we fear that this philosophy, while it endeavours to limit our enquiries to common life, should ever undermine the reasonings of common life, and carry its doubts so far as to destroy all action, as well as speculation. Nature will always maintain her rights, and prevail in the end over any abstract reasoning whatsoever. Though we should conclude, for instance, as in the foregoing section, that, in all reasonings from experience, there is a step taken by the mind which is not supported by any argument or process of the understanding; there is no danger that these reasonings, on which almost all knowledge depends, will ever be affected by such a discovery. If the mind be not engaged by argument to make this step, it must be induced by some other principle of equal weight and authority; and that principle will preserve its influence as long as human nature remains the same. What that principle is may well be worth the pains of enquiry.

Suppose a person, though endowed with the strongest faculties of reason and reflection, to be brought on a sudden into this world; he would, indeed, immediately observe a continual succession of objects, and one event following another; but he would not be able to discover anything farther. He would not, at first, by any reasoning, be able to reach the idea of cause and effect; since the particular powers, by which all natural operations are performed, never appear to the senses; nor is it reasonable to conclude, merely because one event, in one instance, precedes another, that therefore the one is the cause, the other the effect. Their conjunction may be arbitrary and casual. There may be no reason to infer the existence of one from the appearance of the other. And in a word, such a person, without more experience, could never employ his conjecture or reasoning concerning any matter of fact, or be assured of anything beyond what was immediately present to his memory and senses.

Suppose, again, that he has acquired more experience, and has lived so long in the world as to have observed familiar objects or events to be constantly conjoined together; what is the consequence of this experience? He immediately infers the existence of one object from the appearance of the other. Yet he has not, by all his experience, acquired any idea or knowledge of the secret power by which the one object produces the other; nor is it, by any process of reasoning, he is engaged to draw this inference. But still he finds himself determined to draw it: And though he should be convinced that his understanding has no part in the operation, he would nevertheless continue in the same course of thinking. There is some other principle which determines him to form such a conclusion.

This principle is Custom or Habit. For wherever the repetition of any particular act or operation produces a propensity to renew the same act or operation, without being impelled by any reasoning or process of the understanding, we always say, that this propensity is the effect of *Custom*. By employing that word, we pretend not to have given the ultimate reason of such a propensity. We only point out a principle of human nature, which is universally acknowledged, and which is well known by its effects. Perhaps we can push our enquiries no farther, or pretend to give the cause of this cause; but must rest contented with it as the ultimate principle, which we can assign, of all our conclusions from experience. It is sufficient satisfaction, that we can go so far, without repining at the narrowness of our faculties because they will carry us no farther. And it is certain we here advance a very intelligible proposition at least, if not a true one, when we assert that, after the constant conjunction of two objects—heat and flame, for instance, weight and solidity—we are determined by custom alone to expect the one from the appearance of the other. This hypothesis seems even the only one which explains the difficulty, why we draw, from a thousand instances, an inference which we are not able to draw from one instance, that is, in no respect, different from them. Reason is incapable of any such variation. The conclusions which it draws from considering one circle are the same which it would form upon surveying all the circles in the universe. But no man, having seen only one body move after being impelled by another, could infer that every other body will move after a like impulse. All inferences from experience, therefore, are effects of custom, not of reasoning.[3]

Custom, then, is the great guide of human life. It is that principle alone which renders our experience useful to us, and makes us expect, for the future, a similar train of events with those which have appeared in the past. Without the influence of custom, we should be entirely ignorant of every matter of fact beyond what is immediately present to the memory and senses. We should never know how to adjust means to ends, or to employ our natural powers in the production of any effect. There would be an end at once of all action, as well as of the chief part of speculation.

But here it may be proper to remark, that though our conclusions from experience carry us beyond our memory and senses, and assure us of matters of fact which happened in the most distant places and most remote ages, yet some fact must always be present to the senses or memory, from which we may first proceed in drawing these conclusions. A man, who should find in a desert country the remains of pompous buildings, would conclude that the country had, in ancient times, been cultivated by civilized inhabitants; but did nothing of this nature occur to him, he could never form such an inference. We learn the events of former ages from history; but then we must peruse the volumes in which this instruction is contained, and thence carry up our inferences from one testimony to another, till we arrive at the eyewitnesses and spectators of these distant events. In a word, if we proceed not upon some fact, present to the memory or senses, our reasonings would be merely hypothetical; and however the particular links might be connected with each other, the whole chain of inferences would have nothing to support

[3] A long footnote has been omitted here. Hume's aim in this footnote is to show that even where we make a distinction between conclusions drawn on the basis of reason and those drawn on the basis of experience, we must recognize that the former require a man of experience as well, a man who has made some observations and learned from experience.—Ed.

it, nor could we ever, by its means, arrive at the knowledge of any real existence. If I ask why you believe any particular matter of fact, which you relate, you must tell me some reason; and this reason will be some other fact, connected with it. But as you cannot proceed after this manner, *in infinitum,* you must at last terminate in some fact, which is present to your memory or senses; or must allow that your belief is entirely without foundation.

What, then, is the conclusion of the whole matter? A simple one; though, it must be confessed, pretty remote from the common theories of philosophy. All belief of matter of fact or real existence is derived merely from some object, present to the memory or senses, and a customary conjunction, between that and some other object. Or in other words; having found, in many instances, that any two kinds of objects—flame and heat, snow and cold—have always been conjoined together; if flame or snow be presented anew to the senses, the mind is carried by custom to expect heat or cold, and to *believe* that such a quality does exist, and will discover itself upon a nearer approach. This belief is the necessary result of placing the mind in such circumstances. It is an operation of the soul, when we are so situated, as unavoidable as to feel the passion of love, when we receive benefits; or hatred, when we meet with injuries. All these operations are a species of natural instincts, which no reasoning or process of the thought and understanding is able either to produce or to prevent.

At this point, it would be very allowable for us to stop our philosophical researches. In most questions we can never make a single step farther; and in all questions we must terminate here at last, after our most restless and curious enquiries. But still our curiosity will be pardonable, perhaps commendable, if it carry us on to still farther researches, and make us examine more accurately the nature of this *belief,* and of the *customary conjunction,* whence it is derived. By this means we may meet with some explications and analogies that will give satisfaction; at least to such as love the abstract sciences, and can be entertained with speculations, which, however accurate, may still retain a degree of doubt and uncertainty.

H. H. PRICE

Some Considerations About Belief

In knowledge, the mind is directly confronted with a certain fact or with a certain particular. Knowledge is by definition infallible, though of course it need not be exhaustive. But it cannot intelligibly be called true, because the alternatives *true or false* have no application to it. Nor can it be called either active or passive, despite the opinion of writers on the history of Philosophy. For even to ask the question whether it is active or passive (the question which the Rationalists are supposed to have answered in one way and the Empiricists in another and Kant in both) is to commit an absurdity, the absurdity of regarding knowledge as a causal relation.[1] Knowledge is something ultimate and not further analysable. It is simply the situation in which some entity or some fact is directly present to consciousness. The fact may of course be of the form "that p entails q". The knowledge is then called inferring. But it is none the less direct, though its object is in this case more complex.

Belief on the other hand is always fallible. What I believe need not be the case, however firmly I believe it, and however strong the evidence I have for it. Moreover, there is a certain *indirectness* about belief. When I believe truly, there is a fact which makes my belief true. But this fact is not itself present to my mind. That which is present to my mind is something else, something which in this case corresponds to or accords with a fact, but in other cases does not. (It seems to me that many critics of the Correspondence Theory of Truth [2] fail to notice that this theory is only meant to apply to belief and not at all to knowledge. A correspondence theory of knowledge would of course be absurd.)

From H. H. Price, "Some Considerations About Belief," *Proceedings of the Aristotelian Society,* Vol. **XXV** (1935), pp. 229–240. Reprinted by courtesy of the Editor of The Aristotelian Society. [The selection included in this anthology is the major part of the essay by Price.]

[1] I am not saying that the philosophers of the 17th and 18th centuries themselves committed this absurdity, but only that it has been thrust upon them by writers of the history of philosophy.

[2] The "Correspondence Theory of Truth" (found in Aristotle) says that a proposition is true if it "corresponds to" whatever is the case. Price's point is that it is tautologous if taken as a definition of knowledge, but that it states what we mean by "true belief."—Ed.

The distinction between knowledge and false belief is obvious. That between knowledge and true belief is sometimes denied or questioned. Perhaps the following example will make it clear. Suppose I am puzzled about something. Then I myself can *know* by introspection that I am puzzled. Another man observing my behaviour, and noticing the frown on my face and the groans that I utter, can *believe* that I am puzzled; and his belief will be true. But it is obvious that *his* relation to my puzzlement is quite different from my relation to it. I do not mean merely that I am the subject or owner of the puzzlement and he is not. What I mean is that the puzzlement is not directly present to his consciousness, whereas it *is* directly present to mine. Something is indeed present to his consciousness, whatever that something should be called: not, however, the puzzlement itself, but something else which corresponds or accords with it,—something which could perfectly well have been present to his mind even if the puzzlement had not existed in me at all.

It follows that it is impossible to know and to believe the same thing at the same time. If I know that A is B, I cannot at the same time believe that A is B, and if I believe it I cannot at the same time know it; though of course I might believe it at one time and know it at another.

This consequence has sometimes, I think, been denied. It is thought by some philosophers that whenever we make a statement a peculiar sort of mental act occurs which the statement expresses. (The statement would not of course *state* that this act is occurring, but it would express it, in the sense in which a groan expresses distress or a smile expresses pleasure.) This mental act is sometimes called *asserting*. Others call it *judging*. Now sometimes one knows that which one is stating, though often one does not; consequently it will be possible on this view both to know that A is B and at the same time to assert or judge that A is B. Now some people who hold this view have chosen to use the word "believe" as a synonym for "judge" or "assert". It follows that according to them one can know that something is the case and at the same time believe it.

Now for my part I very much doubt . . . whether this supposed act of asserting or judging exists at all. There is indeed the act of formulating something in words or other symbols. And one can distinguish this act of inventing a statement from the subsequent act of uttering it or writing it down. It is, however, a practical act, none the less so for being private to the doer; if you like, an artistic one. It is certainly not a cognitive act, as asserting or judging is supposed to be. Also when I know some fact there are various emotional attitudes which I might have towards it, such as astonishment or fear or distress. Perhaps there is even some one emotional attitude which I always have whenever I state some fact which I know, an attitude of respect or deference or submission to this fact. And perhaps my statement always *expresses* this emotion as well as *signifying* the fact itself. But is there any *cognitive* act or attitude expressed by the statement over and above the mere knowing? I cannot see that there is. The fact is present to my consciousness, and I fabricate a sentence or other complex symbol to signify this fact. What more is there in it than this?

However, suppose there is this cognitive act which occurs whenever I make a statement and which the statement expresses. Even so, it seems to me very unfortunate to call it *belief*. For we want the word "belief" for something else, for that mental attitude, other than knowing and contrasted with it, which I tried to describe above: for that something which is fallible and indirect, whereas knowing is infallible and direct. And this I think is what the word belief is ordinarily used to mean. We say for instance "I don't know that he is in Oxford, but I believe he is": whereas we never say "I know he is in Oxford *and* I believe he is". If anyone objects to this usage, I must ask him to find another word for this non-knowing and fallible cognitive attitude; at any rate it certainly exists and we are all very familiar with it.

We may now proceed to give a prima facie analysis of belief, having shown how it differs from knowing. First we distinguish two elements in belief: (1) the *entertaining* of a proposition, (2) the *assenting to* or *adopting of* that proposition. Before going further we must say something more about each.

With regard to (1), I am of course aware that the phrase "to entertain a proposition" is a stumbling-block to many philosophers. I shall be asked whether I hold with Bolzano and Meinong [3] that propositions are real entities independent of the mind, existing or subsisting in a world of their own, distinct from the world of facts. I reply that I use the phrase "entertaining a proposition" in an en-

---

[3] For information about these two philosophers and some readings from Meinong, see R. M. Chisholm, *Realism and the Background of Phenomenology* (New York: The Free Press of Glencoe, 1960).—Ed.

tirely non-committal way, to stand for an experience which we are all perfectly familiar with. Everyone knows what it is to understand a statement, without either believing or disbelieving what is stated. For instance, we can all understand the statements "A thunderstorm is now occurring in Siam" or "there will be a general election in September", and we can understand them without either belief or disbelief. The understanding of such a statement is something different from merely hearing or reading the words which compose the statement: it is what I call entertaining a proposition. Or again, everyone knows what it is to think of A "as" being B, without either believing or disbelieving that A *is* B, and without knowing that A is B or that it is not. I do not know whether Smith is or is not brushing his hair at this moment, and I neither believe that he is doing so nor disbelieve it (why should I?). But I can and do think of him "as" brushing his hair at this moment. This situation where we think of something "as" such and such is what I am calling entertaining a proposition. About the nature of this act and of its object (whatever names they are called by) various theories have been suggested, of which the Bolzano-Meinong theory is one but only one. I do not intend to discuss any of these theories: not because I think the topic unimportant—it has been rightly said by a Cambridge philosopher that entertaining is "the most mental thing that we do"—but because the differences between them are irrelevant to the problems which I do wish to discuss. Whichever of these theories we hold, these problems will still arise.

In order to make clear what was meant by the word "entertain" I had to take this act in isolation, so to speak, and consider the case where we understand a statement or think of A as B without either belief or disbelief. But in point of fact entertaining does not as a rule occur alone. We usually take up some *further* attitude towards that which we entertain. Thus entertaining is usually an element in a more complex mental attitude. It is for instance contained in doubting, questioning, supposing; it also forms part of certain emotional attitudes, as when I hope that it will be fine tomorrow, or fear that it will rain, or am surprised at a story which I read in the newspaper. In particular, believing and disbelieving contain entertaining. It can occur without them (as we have said) but not they without it.

This brings us to the second element in our prima facie theory of belief, the element of assent or adoption. To make clear what this is, we must go back a little and consider the process which precedes the forming of a belief. We begin, according to this theory, by entertaining *several* propositions (at least two) which are mutually exclusive. Let us suppose that we have lost the cat. We entertain the propositions that the cat is in the cupboard, that it is in the coalscuttle, that it is behind the sofa. We consider or wonder about these three propositions, and as yet we believe none of them. But presently we hear a noise from the direction of the cupboard, and forthwith we *assent to* or *adopt* the proposition that the cat is in the cupboard, and *dissent from* or *reject* the other two alternative propositions.

It is difficult to give a further account of this process of assenting. It seems to me to consist of two elements, one volitional and one emotional. On the one hand, it is analogous to choice or preference or decision; [4] and it is significant that we say "I decided (or made up my mind) *that* A was B" as well as "I decided (or made up my mind) to do X". When we come out of the state of considering into the state of assent we seem as it were to be coming down on one side of the fence, or to be taking a plunge. At first we were neutral as between the alternatives. But now we have come to be in favour of one and against the rest. On the other hand, assent also has an emotional side. When we believe something, we feel a feeling of *sureness* or *confidence* with regard to it. As we say, we feel comfortable about it.

The first of these factors in assent admits of no degrees. Either we decide in favour of p and against its alternatives q and r, or we do not. We may indeed revoke our decision later; but still, at the time of its occurrence it must occur wholly or not at all. But the emotional factor may have all sorts of degrees. "I rather think that A is B" expresses a very mild degree of confidence. "I suppose" or "I expect" are often used colloquially, though inaccurately, to express a slightly greater degree of it than this. "I think" expresses still more. And "I am sure" or "quite sure" or "I feel certain" express a very high degree of confidence. Perhaps the lower half of the scale might be called *opinion* and the upper half *conviction;* and the upper limit might be called *absolute conviction.*

In the instance we took above, our assent was assent *upon evidence;* we had a *reason* for believing as we did. We assented to the proposition that the cat is in the cupboard because we heard a

---

[4] Cf. Descartes' account of judgement.

noise coming from that direction, and no noises from the sofa or the coal-scuttle. But what is meant by "having evidence for a proposition p", or "having a reason for" believing it? According to the present theory, it means (a) *knowing* some fact and (b) *knowing* that this fact makes p more probable than its alternatives. Thus, according to this theory, belief always contains knowing. And this is one of the most striking points about the theory; we shall return to it later.

In this connexion, a sharp distinction is drawn between the *reasons* for a belief and the *cause* or psychological origin of it. And it is suggested that no enquiry into the psychological origins of a belief—for instance into the wishes or emotions or habits or traditions which caused people to believe a certain proposition p, has any tendency to show either that p is true or it is false. If we wish to discover whether it is true or false, we must simply consider the reasons for and against it. The difficulty here is that having a reason is itself a kind of cause. Knowing is a physical event, no less than wishing, and like others it can have effects. It would be clearer if we said that assent can be determined in two distinct ways: (a) cognitively, by the knowing of evidence in favour of the proposition assented to, (b) emotionally and volitionally. These two cause-factors vary independently; sometimes one predominates, and sometimes the other. But in all belief both must be present in some degree. Assent could not be entirely determined by the knowing of evidence; for at least we must be *interested* in the propositions between which the evidence is to decide, otherwise we should never consider them at all. But if this is the sole effect of the emotional and volitional factors, our belief is as rational as any belief can be.

Could there on the other hand be an entirely *ir*rational belief, where assent is entirely determined by our emotions and volitions, and not at all by the knowing of evidence? I do not think that there could. Here we have to distinguish two possible cases. Suppose, for simplicity, that there are only two alternatives, p and q. And suppose that we have a great deal of evidence for p, and very little evidence for q. Can we in spite of this assent to q, owing to our hopes or fears or wishes? It seems to me that we cannot do so directly. But we may indirectly. For the wishes, etc., may divert our attention away from the evidence for p and restrict it to the evidence for q. The other case is that in which there is no evidence at all on either side, as when we come to a fork in a road, and have no evidence as to which of the two branch-roads is the right one. Here it seems to me that assent, and therefore belief, is impossible. We can only *decide to act as if* road A was the right one. But we do not on that account believe it. For we feel no confidence about its being the right one. It is true that some philosophers have tried to identify assenting to p with deciding to act as if p was true. But it is clear from this case that we can decide to act thus without believing p at all. Not only so. We sometimes decide to act as if p was true when we *dis*believe it, or even because we disbelieve it: as when we act as if a particular scientific or archaeological theory were true in order to convince someone else that it is false.

So far we have distinguished the following four factors in the situation called "believing p":—

(1) Entertaining p together with one or more alternative propositions q and r.
(2) Knowing a fact (or set of facts) F, which is relevant to p, q and r.
(3) Knowing that F makes p more likely than q or r, i.e. having more evidence for p than for q or r.
(4) Assenting to p; which in turn includes
   (a) the preferring of p to q and r;
   (b) the feeling a certain degree of confidence with regard to p.

An interesting consequence follows. It is obvious that any belief may be mistaken (this is indeed part of the definition of belief). However much evidence we have for a proposition, and however confident we feel about it, it may still be false. Thus, in our example above, the noise in the cupboard may have been made by a rat or a small boy, and the cat may be under the sofa after all. But must the believer himself be aware of this possibility? It seems clear that according to the above analysis he must be. For he knows that there are alternatives to p. He knows that his evidence is incomplete, i.e. that there *are* other relevant facts whose *specific nature* he does not know. And he knows that F only makes p *more likely* than q and r, but does not *prove* p, nor disprove q and r.

Yet there certainly is a state of mind which we are tempted to call belief where we are *not* aware of the possibility that we may be mistaken. This is the state which the present theory calls *taking for granted* or *acceptance,* or with Cook Wilson, *being under an impression that.* (Professor Prichard, I believe, calls it "thinking without question".) To refuse to call it belief may seem somewhat artificial; but it does differ in a very important way from what we have hitherto been calling belief.

The traditional example of taking for granted is as follows. We see a man walking in front of us in the street having red hair and a dark blue overcoat. Without any weighing of evidence or any consideration of alternatives we straightway jump to the conclusion that it is our friend Smith. We walk up to him and slap him on the back. And then we discover that it is not Smith at all, but a perfect stranger.

Obviously this is quite different from the case discussed before. No doubt we should apologize and say "I am sorry, I *thought* you were Smith". But "thought" does not here mean "assented upon evidence with a mild degree of confidence". We may indeed be tempted to say, as Mr. Russell does about a similar case, that our apologetic statement is simply false; that we were not *thinking* at all, but merely behaving. And sometimes this is so. But not always. It seems necessary to distinguish between this purely behaviouristic *quasi-acceptance* (if we may call it so) and acceptance proper, where we do think, at least in one sense of that ambiguous word. In acceptance proper we do entertain the proposition "this man is Smith", and entertaining is certainly thinking. But we do not assent to it. For assent involves preference, as we have seen, and this requires the entertaining of at least two alternatives. One prefers something to something else. But here there is no something else. No alternative occurs to our mind at all. What happens is that *we do not dissent* from the proposition. Likewise it is not that we feel a certain degree of sureness with regard to the proposition. What happens is that *we do not feel unsure*. We entertain it without any doubt or question. This differs from the state of "suspending judgement" about a proposition. There we suppress our doubts and questions by a deliberate and often painful effort. But here no doubt or question arises in us, so we do not have to suppress it. We just surrender ourselves to the proposition in a childlike and effortless way. Accordingly we are quite unaware of the fact that the proposition may after all not be true. And if it turns out false, we feel a peculiarly disconcerting and painful shock, quite different from the mild surprise and disappointment which results from the unmasking of an ordinary false belief. It is like the shock of being suddenly waked from a dream.

Having said what acceptance is, we must now ask how it comes about. Assent as we saw is determined by two independent factors, the knowing of evidence on the one side, volitional and emotional factors on the other. Obviously volitional and emotional factors play a part in determining acceptance too. If we want to see Smith, we shall be more likely to take the stranger to be Smith.[5] (Likewise if we are afraid of seeing him.) We might, indeed, be tempted to say that acceptance is wholly determined by volition and emotion; but this cannot be right. We do not mistake a wall or an elephant for Smith, nor even a scarecrow, however much we want (or fear) to see him. We have to see or hear or touch something which resembles him fairly closely. Thus our acceptance is partly caused by a cognitive process, namely, by what is called "association of ideas". Only the association is not of course between "ideas" (if indeed that word means anything); it is between two sets of characteristics —the having red hair and a blue overcoat on the one side, and the remaining Smith-characteristics on the other. This association plays the same part in acceptance as the awareness of favourable evidence played in the case of belief proper. (In the purely behaviouristic quasi-acceptance the association is replaced by a conditioned reflex, connecting a certain kind of stimulus to the sense-organs with a certain kind of bodily movement.)

But here a curious complication arises. Even in acceptance, it may seem that there is *evidence* for the accepted proposition. The association has arisen because Smith does have red hair and does habitually wear a blue overcoat. But if so, the fact that this man here is red haired and wears a blue overcoat is evidence that he is Smith (its being so is of course compatible with his being in fact somebody else: evidence is not proof). But if we have got evidence for the proposition which we accept, is there really any difference between acceptance and belief after all? To clear up this point we must distinguish between the consciousness of something which is in fact evidence, and the *using* it as evidence: for instance, between perceiving something which does *in fact* make p likely and *recognizing* that it makes p likely. It is this recognizing or using which is absent in acceptance and present in belief proper. We can convince ourselves by introspection that it is absent, and we can also produce an

[5] Yet curiously enough, we must not be *too* desirous (or fearful) of seeing Smith. For if we were, we should be more careful. Our anxiety would make us consider alternatives and weigh evidence, and we should have belief proper, instead of just jumping to a conclusion.

argument to show that it must be. For if we recognize that F makes p likely, we must also recognize that p may, after all, be false, and some alternative proposition true; and this recognition is absent in acceptance, though present in belief. Indeed its absence is the differentia of acceptance, as we saw at first. Now according to ordinary usage we are only said to "have" evidence for p when we *recognize* that such and such a fact makes p likely. Thus it is not true that in acceptance (or taking for granted) we have evidence for what we accept; though we could have it, if we aroused ourselves from our unquestioning state of mind, and considered critically what we are already conscious of.

DAVID HUME

Belief as a Unique Feeling

Nothing is more free than the imagination of man; and though it cannot exceed that original stock of ideas furnished by the internal and external senses, it has unlimited power of mixing, compounding, separating, and dividing these ideas, in all the varieties of fiction and vision. It can feign a train of events, with all the appearance of reality, ascribe to them a particular time and place, conceive them as existent, and paint them out to itself with every circumstance, that belongs to any historical fact, which it believes with the greatest certainty. Wherein, therefore, consists the difference between such a fiction and belief? It lies not merely in any peculiar idea, which is annexed to such a conception as commands our assent, and which is wanting to every known fiction. For as the mind has authority over all its ideas, it could voluntarily annex this particular idea to any fiction, and consequently be able to believe whatever it pleases; contrary to what we find by daily experience. We can, in our conception, join the head of a man to the body of a horse; but it is not in our power to believe that such an animal has ever really existed.

It follows, therefore, that the difference between *fiction* and *belief* lies in some sentiment or feeling, which is annexed to the latter, not to the former, and which depends not on the will, nor can be commanded at pleasure. It must be excited by nature, like all other sentiments; and must arise from the particular situation, in which the mind is placed at any particular juncture. Whenever any object is presented to the memory or senses, it immediately, by the force of custom, carries the imagination to conceive that object, which is usually conjoined to it; and this conception is attended with a feeling or sentiment, different from the loose reveries of the fancy. In this consists the whole nature of belief. For as there is no matter of fact which we believe so firmly that we cannot conceive the contrary, there would be no difference between the conception assented to and that which is rejected, were it not for some sentiment which distinguishes the one from the other. If I see a billiard-ball moving towards another, on a smooth table, I can easily conceive it to stop

From Hume, *op. cit.*, Sec. V, Part II, pp. 47–55.

upon contact. This conception implies no contradiction; but still it feels very differently from that conception by which I represent to myself the impulse and the communication of motion from one ball to another.

Were we to attempt a *definition* of this sentiment, we should, perhaps, find it a very difficult, if not an impossible task; in the same manner as if we should endeavour to define the feeling of cold or passion of anger, to a creature who never had any experience of these sentiments. Belief is the true and proper name of this feeling; and no one is ever at a loss to know the meaning of that term; because every man is every moment conscious of the sentiment represented by it. It may not, however, be improper to attempt a *description* of this sentiment; in hopes we may, by that means, arrive at some analogies, which may afford a more perfect explication of it. I say, then, that belief is nothing but a more vivid, lively, forcible, firm, steady conception of an object, than what the imagination alone is ever able to attain. This variety of terms, which may seem so unphilosophical, is intended only to express that act of the mind, which renders realities, or what is taken for such, more present to us than fictions, causes them to weigh more in the thought, and gives them a superior influence on the passions and imagination. Provided we agree about the thing, it is needless to dispute about the terms. The imagination has the command over all its ideas, and can join and mix and vary them, in all the ways possible. It may conceive fictitious objects with all the circumstances of place and time. It may set them, in a manner, before our eyes, in their true colours, just as they might have existed. But as it is impossible that this faculty of imagination can ever, of itself, reach belief, it is evident that belief consists not in the peculiar nature or order of ideas, but in the *manner* of their conception, and in their *feeling* to the mind. I confess, that it is impossible perfectly to explain this feeling or manner of conception. We may make use of words which express something near it. But its true and proper name, as we observed before, is *belief;* which is a term that every one sufficiently understands in common life. And in philosophy, we can go no farther than assert, that *belief* is something felt by the mind, which distinguishes the ideas of the judgement from the fictions of the imagination. It gives them more weight and influence; makes them appear of greater importance; enforces them in the mind; and renders them the governing principle of our actions. I hear at present, for instance, a person's voice, with whom I am acquainted; and the sound comes as from the next room. This impression of my senses immediately conveys my thought to the person, together with all the surrounding objects. I paint them out to myself as existing at present, with the same qualities and relations, of which I formerly knew them possessed. These ideas take faster hold of my mind than ideas of an enchanted castle. They are very different to the feeling, and have a much greater influence of every kind, either to give pleasure or pain, joy or sorrow.

Let us, then, take in the whole compass of this doctrine, and allow, that the sentiment of belief is nothing but a conception more intense and steady than what attends the mere fictions of the imagination, and that this *manner* of conception arises from a customary conjunction of the object with something present to the memory or senses: I believe that it will not be difficult, upon these suppositions, to find other operations of the mind analogous to it, and to trace up these phenomena to principles still more general.

We have already observed that nature has established connexions among particular ideas, and that no sooner one idea occurs to our thoughts than it introduces its correlative, and carries our attention towards it, by a gentle and insensible movement. These principles of connexion or association we have reduced to three, namely *Resemblance, Contiguity* and *Causation;* which are the only bonds that unite our thoughts together, and beget that regular train of reflection or discourse, which, in a greater or less degree, takes place among all mankind. Now here arises a question, on which the solution of the present difficulty will depend. Does it happen, in all these relations, that, when one of the objects is presented to the senses or memory, the mind is not only carried to the conception of the correlative, but reaches a steadier and stronger conception of it than what otherwise it would have been able to attain? This seems to be the case with that belief which arises from the relation of cause and effect. And if the case be the same with the other relations or principles of associations, this may be established as a general law, which takes place in all the operations of the mind.

We may, therefore, observe, as the first experiment to our present purpose, that, upon the appearance of the picture of an absent friend, our idea of him is evidently enlivened by the *resemblance,* and that every passion, which that idea occasions, whether of joy or sorrow, acquires new force and vigour. In producing this effect, there concur both a relation and a present impression. Where the picture bears him no resemblance, at least was not intended for him, it never so much as conveys our thought to him: And where it is absent, as well as the person, though the mind may pass from the thought of the one to that of the other, it feels its idea to be rather weakened than enlivened by that transition. We take a pleasure in viewing the picture of a friend, when it is set before us; but when it is removed, rather choose to consider him directly than by reflection in an image, which is equally distant and obscure.

The ceremonies of the Roman Catholic religion may be considered as instances of the same nature. The devotees of that superstition usually plead in excuse for the mummeries, with which they are upbraided, that they feel the good effect of those external motions, and postures, and actions, in enlivening their devotion and quickening their fervour, which otherwise would decay, if directed entirely to distant and immaterial objects. We shadow out the objects of our faith, say they, in sensible types and images, and render them more present to us by the immediate presence of these types, than it is possible for us to do merely by an intellectual view and contemplation. Sensible objects have always a greater influence on the fancy than any other; and this influence they readily convey to those ideas to which they are related, and which they resemble. I shall only infer from these practices, and this reasoning, that the effect of resemblance in enlivening the ideas is very common; and as in every case a resemblance and a present impression must concur, we are abundantly supplied with experiments to prove the reality of the foregoing principle.

We may add force to these experiments by others of a different kind, in considering the effects of *contiguity* as well as of *resemblance*. It is certain that distance diminishes the force of every idea, and that, upon our approach to any object; though it does not discover itself to our senses; it operates upon the mind with an influence, which imitates an immediate impression. The thinking on any object readily transports the mind to what is contiguous; but it is only the actual presence of an object, that transports it with a superior vivacity. When I am a few miles from home, whatever relates to it touches me more nearly than when I am two hundred leagues distant; though even at that distance the reflecting on any thing in the neighbourhood of my friends or family naturally produces an idea of them. But as in this latter case, both the objects of the mind are ideas; notwithstanding there is an easy transition between them; that transition alone is not able to give a superior vivacity to any of the ideas, for want of some immediate impression.

No one can doubt but causation has the same influence as the other two relations of resemblance and contiguity. Superstitious people are fond of the reliques of saints and holy men, for the same reason, that they seek after types or images, in order to enliven their devotion, and give them a more intimate and strong conception of those exemplary lives, which they desire to imitate. Now it is evident, that one of the best reliques, which a devotee could procure, would be the handywork of a saint; and if his cloaths and furniture are ever to be considered in this light, it is because they were once at his disposal, and were moved and affected by him; in which respect they are to be considered as imperfect effects, and as connected with him by a shorter chain of consequences than any of those, by which we learn the reality of his existence.

Suppose, that the son of a friend, who had been long dead or absent, were presented to us; it is evident, that this object would instantly revive its correlative idea, and recall to our thoughts all past intimacies and familiarities, in more lively colours than they would otherwise have appeared to us. This is another phaenomenon, which seems to prove the principle above mentioned.

We may observe, that, in these phaenomena, the belief of the correlative object is always presupposed; without which the relation could have no effect. The influence of the picture supposes, that we *believe* our friend to have once existed. Contiguity to home can never excite our ideas of home, unless we *believe* that it really exists. Now I assert, that this belief, where it reaches beyond the memory or senses, is of a similar nature, and arises from similar causes, with the transition of thought and vivacity of conception here explained. When I throw a piece of dry wood into a fire, my mind is immediately carried to conceive, that it augments, not extinguishes the flame. This transition of thought from the cause to the effect proceeds not from reason. It derives its origin altogether from custom and experience. And as it first begins from an object, present to the senses, it renders the idea or conception of flame more strong and lively than any loose, floating reverie of the imagination. That idea arises immediately. The thought moves instantly towards it, and conveys to it all that force of conception, which is derived from the impression present to the senses. When a sword is levelled at my breast, does not the idea of wound and pain strike me more strongly, than when a glass of wine is presented to me, even though by accident this idea should occur after the appearance of the latter object? But what is there in this whole matter to cause such a strong conception, except only a present object and a customary transition to the idea of another object, which we have been accustomed to conjoin with the former? This is the whole operation of the mind, in all our conclusions concerning matter of fact and existence; and it is a satisfaction to find some analogies, by which it may be explained. The transition from a present object does in all cases give strength and solidity to the related idea.

Here, then, is a kind of pre-established harmony between the course of nature and the succession of our ideas; and though the powers and forces, by which the former is governed, be wholly unknown to us; yet our thoughts and conceptions have still, we find, gone on in the same train with the other works of nature. Custom is that principle, by which this correspondence has been effected; so necessary to the subsistence of our species, and the regulation of our conduct, in every circumstance and occurrence of human life. Had not the presence of an object, instantly excited the idea of those objects, commonly conjoined with it, all our knowledge must have been limited to the narrow sphere of our memory and senses; and we should never have been able to adjust means to ends, or employ our natural powers, either to the producing of good, or avoiding of evil. Those, who delight in the discovery and contemplation of *final causes*, have here ample subject to employ their wonder and admiration.

I shall add, for a further confirmation of the foregoing theory, that, as this operation of the mind, by which we infer like effects from like causes, and *vice versa*, is so essential to the subsistence of all human creatures, it is not probable, that it could be trusted to the fallacious deductions of our reason, which is slow in its operations; appears not, in any degree, during the first years of infancy; and at best is, in every age and period of human life, extremely liable to error and mistake. It is more conformable to the ordinary wisdom of nature to secure so necessary an act of the mind, by some instinct or mechanical tendency, which may be infallible in its operations, may discover itself at the first appearance of life and thought, and may be independent of all the laboured deductions of the understanding. As nature has taught us the use of our limbs, without giving us the knowledge of the muscles and nerves, by which they are actuated; so has she implanted in us an instinct, which carries forward the thought in a correspondent course to that which she has established among external objects; though we are ignorant of those powers and forces on which this regular course and succession of objects totally depends.

PART III

Normative Epistemology

RENÉ DESCARTES

The Criterion of Certainty

René Descartes (1596–1650). The important French philosopher, whose Meditations *became the subject of extended debates and exchanges by philosophers in France and England, he is generally credited with turning modern philosophy toward the problems of self-knowledge.*

MEDITATION I: OF THE THINGS WHICH MAY BE BROUGHT WITHIN THE SPHERE OF THE DOUBTFUL

It is now some years since I detected how many were the false beliefs that I had from my earliest youth admitted as true, and how doubtful was everything I had since constructed on this basis; and from that time I was convinced that I must once for all seriously undertake to rid myself of all the opinions which I had formerly accepted, and commence to build anew from the foundation, if I wanted to establish any firm and permanent structure in the sciences. But as this enterprise appeared to be a very great one, I waited until I had attained an age so mature that I could not hope that at any later date I should be better fitted to execute my design. This reason caused me to delay so long that I should feel that I was doing wrong were I to occupy in deliberation the time that yet

From René Descartes, *Meditations on First Philosophy*, in *Philosophical Works*, Vol. I, ed. and trans. E. S. Haldane and G. R. T. Ross (London: Cambridge University Press, 1931), pp. 144–150. Used by permission of Cambridge University Press.

remains to me for action. To-day, then, since very opportunely for the plan I have in view I have delivered my mind from every care [and am happily agitated by no passions] and since I have procured for myself an assured leisure in a peaceable retirement, I shall at last seriously and freely address myself to the general upheaval of all my former opinions.

Now for this object it is not necessary that I should show that all of these are false—I shall perhaps never arrive at this end. But inasmuch as reason already persuades me that I ought no less carefully to withhold my assent from matters which are not entirely certain and indubitable than from those which appear to me manifestly to be false, if I am able to find in each one some reason to doubt, this will suffice to justify my rejecting the whole. And for that end it will not be requisite that I should examine each in particular, which would be an endless undertaking; for owing to the fact that the destruction of the foundations of necessity brings with it the downfall of the rest of the edifice, I shall only in the first place attack those principles upon which all my former opinions rested.

All that up to the present time I have accepted as most true and certain I have learned either from the senses or through the senses; but it is sometimes proved to me that these senses are deceptive, and it is wiser not to trust entirely to any thing by which we have once been deceived.

But it may be that although the senses sometimes deceive us concerning things which are hardly perceptible, or very far away, there are yet many others to be met with as to which we cannot reasonably have any doubt, although we recognise them by their means. For example, there is the fact that I am here, seated by the fire, attired in a dressing gown, having this paper in my hands and other similar matters. And how could I deny that these hands and this body are mine, were it not perhaps that I compare myself to certain persons, devoid of sense, whose cerebella are so troubled and clouded by the violent vapours of black bile, that they constantly assure us that they think they are kings when they are really quite poor, or that they are clothed in purple when they are really without covering, or who imagine that they have an earthenware head or are nothing but pumpkins or are made of glass. But they are mad, and I should not be any the less insane were I to follow examples so extravagant.

At the same time I must remember that I am a man, and that consequently I am in the habit of sleeping, and in my dreams representing to myself the same things or sometimes even less probable things, than do those who are insane in their waking moments. How often has it happened to me that in the night I dreamt that I found myself in this particular place, that I was dressed and seated near the fire, whilst in reality I was lying undressed in bed! At this moment it does indeed seem to me that it is with eyes awake that I am looking at this paper; that this head which I move is not asleep, that it is deliberately and of set purpose that I extend my hand and perceive it; what happens in sleep does not appear so clear nor so distinct as does all this. But in thinking over this I remind myself that on many occasions I have in sleep been deceived by similar illusions, and in dwelling carefully on this reflection I see so manifestly that there are no certain indications by which we may clearly distinguish wakefulness from sleep that I am lost in astonishment. And my astonishment is such that it is almost capable of persuading me that I now dream.

Now let us assume that we are asleep and that all these particulars, e.g., that we open our eyes, shake our head, extend our hands, and so on, are but false delusions; and let us reflect that possibly neither our hands nor our whole body are such as they appear to us to be. At the same time we must at least confess that the things which are represented to us in sleep are like painted representations which can only have been formed as the counterparts of something real and true, and that in this way those general things at least, i.e. eyes, a head, hands, and a whole body, are not imaginary things, but things really existent. For, as a matter of fact, painters, even when they study with the greatest skill to represent sirens and satyrs by forms the most strange and extraordinary, cannot give them natures which are entirely new, but merely make a certain medley of the members of different animals; or if their imagination is extragavant enough to invent something so novel that nothing similar has ever before been seen, and that then their work represents a thing purely fictitious and absolutely false, it is certain all the same that the colours of which this is composed are necessarily real. And for the same reason, although these general things, to wit, [a body], eyes, a head, hands, and such like, may be imaginary, we are bound at the same time to confess that there are at least some other objects yet more simple and more universal, which are real and true; and of these just in the same way as with certain real colours, all these images of things which dwell in our thoughts, whether true and real or false and fantastic, are formed.

To such a class of things pertains corporeal nature in general, and its extension, the figure of extended things, their quantity or magnitude and number, as also the place in which they are, the time which measures their duration, and so on.

That is possibly why our reasoning is not unjust when we conclude from this that Physics, Astronomy, Medicine and all other sciences which have as their end the consideration of composite things, are very dubious and uncertain; but that Arithmetic, Geometry and other sciences of that kind which only treat of things that are very simple and very general, without taking great trouble to ascertain whether they are actually existent or not, contain some measure of certainty and an element of the indubitable. For whether I am awake or asleep, two and three together always form five, and the square can never have more than four sides, and it does not seem possible that truths so clear and apparent can be suspected of any falsity [or uncertainty].

Nevertheless I have long had fixed in my mind the belief that an all-powerful God existed by whom I have been created such as I am. But how do I know that He has not brought it to pass that there is no earth, no heaven, no extended body, no magnitude, no place, and that nevertheless [I possess the perceptions of all these things and that] they seem to me to exist just exactly as I now see them? And, besides, as I sometimes imagine that others deceive themselves in the things which they think they know best, how do I know that I am not deceived every time that I add two and three, or count the sides of a square, or judge of things yet simpler, if anything simpler can be imagined? But possibly God has not desired that I should be thus deceived, for He is said to be supremely good. If, however, it is contrary to His goodness to have made me such that I constantly deceive myself, it would also appear to be contrary to His goodness to permit me to be sometimes deceived, and nevertheless I cannot doubt that He does permit this.

There may indeed be those who would prefer to deny the existence of a God so powerful, rather than believe that all other things are uncertain. But let us not oppose them for the present, and grant that all that is here said of a God is a fable; nevertheless in whatever way they suppose that I have arrived at the state of being that I have reached—whether they attribute it to fate or to accident, or make out that it is by a continual succession of antecedents, or by some other method—since to err and deceive oneself is a defect, it is clear that the greater will be the probability of my being so imperfect as to deceive myself ever, as is the Author to whom they assign my origin the less powerful. To these reasons I have certainly nothing to reply, but at the end I feel constrained to confess that there is nothing in all that I formerly believe to be true, of which I cannot in some measure doubt, and that not merely through want of thought or through levity, but for reasons which are very powerful and maturely considered; so that henceforth I ought not the less carefully to refrain from giving credence to these opinions than to that which is manifestly false, if I desire to arrive at any certainty [in the sciences].

But it is not sufficient to have made these remarks, we must also be careful to keep them in mind. For these ancient and commonly held opinions still revert frequently to my mind, long and familiar custom having given them the right to occupy my mind against my inclination and rendered them almost masters of my belief; nor will I ever lose the habit of deferring to them or of placing my confidence in them, so long as I consider them as they really are, i.e. opinions in some measure doubtful, as I have just shown, and at the same time highly probable, so that there is much more reason to believe in than to deny them. That is why I consider that I shall not be acting amiss, if, taking of set purpose a contrary belief, I allow myself to be deceived, and for a certain time pretend that all these opinions are entirely false and imaginary, until at last, having thus balanced my former prejudices with my latter [so that they cannot divert my opinions more to one side than to the other], my judgment will no longer be dominated by bad usage or turned away from the right knowledge of the truth. For I am assured that there can be neither peril nor error in this course, and that I cannot at present yield too much to distrust, since I am not considering the question of action, but only of knowledge.

I shall then suppose, not that God who is supremely good and the fountain of truth, but some evil genius not less powerful than deceitful, has employed his whole energies in deceiving me; I shall consider that the heavens, the earth, colours, figures, sound, and all other external things are nought but the illusions and dreams of which this genius has availed himself in order to lay traps for my credulity; I shall consider myself as having no hands, no eyes, no flesh, no blood, nor any senses, yet falsely believing myself to possess all these things; I shall remain obstinately attached to this idea, and if by this means it is not in my power to arrive at the knowledge of any truth, I may at least do what is in my power [i.e. suspend my judgment], and with firm purpose avoid giving credence to any false thing, or being imposed upon by this arch deceiver, however powerful and deceptive he may be. But this task is a laborious one, and insensibly a certain lassitude leads me into the course of my ordinary life. And just as a captive who in sleep enjoys an imaginary liberty, when he begins to suspect that his liberty is but a dream, fears to awaken, and conspires with these agreeable illusions that the deception may be prolonged, so insensibly of my own accord I fall back into my former opinions, and I dread awakening from this slumber, lest the laborious wakefulness which would follow the tranquillity of this repose should have to be spent not in daylight, but in the excessive darkness of the difficulties which have just been discussed.

MEDITATION II: OF THE NATURE OF THE HUMAN MIND; AND THAT IT IS MORE EASILY KNOWN THAN THE BODY

The Meditation of yesterday filled my mind with so many doubts that it is no longer in my power to forget them. And yet I do not see in what manner I can resolve them; and, just as if I had all of a sudden fallen into very deep water, I am so disconcerted that I can neither make certain of setting my feet on the bottom, nor can I swim and so support myself on the surface. I shall nevertheless make an effort and follow anew the same path as that on which I yesterday entered, i.e. I shall proceed by setting aside all that in which the least doubt could be supposed to exist, just as if I had discovered that it was absolutely false; and I shall ever follow in this road until I have met with something which is certain, or at least, if I can do nothing else, until I have learned for certain that there is nothing in the world that is certain. Archimedes, in order that he might draw the terrestrial globe out of its place, and transport it elsewhere, demanded only that one point should be fixed and immoveable; in the same way I shall have the right to conceive high hopes if I am happy enough to discover one thing only which is certain and indubitable.

I suppose, then, that all the things that I see are false; I persuade myself that nothing has ever existed of all that my fallacious memory represents to me. I consider that I possess no senses; I imagine that body, figure, extension, movement and place are but the fictions of my mind. What, then, can be esteemed as true? Perhaps nothing at all, unless that there is nothing in the world that is certain.

But how can I know there is not something different from those things that I have just considered, of which one cannot have the slightest doubt? Is there not some God, or some other being by whatever name we call it, who puts these reflections into my mind? That is not necessary, for is it not possible that I am capable of producing them myself? I myself, am I not at least something? But I have already denied that I had senses and body. Yet I hesitate, for what follows from that? Am I so dependent on body and senses that I cannot exist without these? But I was persuaded that there was nothing in all the world, that there was no heaven, no earth, that there were no minds, nor any bodies: was I not then likewise persuaded that I did not exist? Not at all; of a surety I myself did exist since I persuaded myself of something [or merely because I thought of something]. But there is some deceiver or other, very powerful and very cunning, who ever employs his ingenuity in deceiving me. Then without doubt I exist also if he deceives me, and let him deceive me as much as he will, he can never cause me to be nothing so long as I think that I am something. So that after having reflected well and carefully examined all things, we must come to the definite conclusion that this proposition: I am, I exist, is necessarily true each time that I pronounce it, or that I mentally conceive it.

RODERICK M. CHISHOLM

The Empirical Criterion

*Roderick M. Chisholm (1916–   ), contemporary American philoso-
pher, Professor at Brown University, is a leading epistemologist and recog-
nized authority on nineteenth-century German philosophy. He has published articles on ethics and theory of knowledge. He is the author of*
Perceiving: A Philosophical Study *(Cornell University Press, 1957) and*
Realism and the Background to Phenomenology *(Free Press, 1960).*

2.

"Adequate evidence" is an *epistemic* term—a term we use in
appraising the epistemic, or cognitive, worth of statements, hypotheses, and beliefs. Making use of the locution, "S ought to place
more confidence in *h* than in *i*," where "S" may be replaced by the
name of a person and "*h*" and "*i*" by the names of propositions,
beliefs, statements, or hypotheses, we may explicate some of our
more important epistemic terms in the following way. "It would be
unreasonable for S to accept *h*" means that S ought to place more confidence in *non-h* than in *h*; "*h* is *acceptable* for S" means that it would
not be unreasonable for S to accept *h*; "*h* is (epistemically) *indifferent*
for S" means that both *h* and *non-h* are acceptable for S; and "S has
adequate evidence for *h*" means that *non-h* is unreasonable for S,
or, in other words, that S ought to place more confidence in *h*
than in *non-h*. By making use of additional locution, "S accepts *h*,"
we may define one important use of "know" and one important use
of "certain." The locution "S *knows that h* is true" could be said
to mean, first, that S accepts *h*, secondly that S has adequate
evidence for *h*, and thirdly, that *h* is true. And "S is *certain* that *h*
is true" could be said to mean, first, that S knows that *h* is true, and,

From Roderick M. Chisholm, "Appear," "Take," and "Evident," *The Journal
of Philosophy,* **LIII** (1956), pp. 722–731. Used by permission of the Directors
of *The Journal of Philosophy* and the author. [The selection included in this
anthology comprises part of the article (Sec. 2, 4, 6, 7, and 8) which the author
contributed to a symposium on "The Concept of Empirical Evidence." For
an elaboration of the notion of a criterion, as well as for some modifications of
suggestions in the article, consult Chisholm's *Perceiving: A Philosophical Study*.]

secondly, that there is no proposition or hypothesis *i* such that S ought to place more confidence in *i* than in *h*.[1]

Our present problem is this: How are we to decide which propositions are evident? Or, more exactly: By means of what principles could our subject S *apply* the locution "S has adequate evidence for *h*"?

In setting this problem for ourselves—the problem of "the criterion"[2]—we do not presuppose, nor should we presuppose, that there are certain principles which people actually think about, or refer to, in order to *decide* whether they have adequate evidence for their beliefs. The grammarian, similarly, may try to describe the conditions under which, say, people use the imperfect tense rather than the past perfect; but, in so doing, he does not mean to imply that, before using this tense, people think about these conditions or try to decide whether or not they apply.

It is important to note that we cannot answer our question by reference solely to the logic of induction and the theory of probability. For the principles of induction and probability will not tell a man which propositions are evident unless he applies them to *premises* which are evident. . . .

4.

Hobbes said, "The inn of evidence has no sign-board." But I suggest that, whenever a man has adequate evidence for some proposition or hypothesis, he is in a state which constitutes a *mark of evidence* for that proposition or hypothesis.

What, then, would be a "mark of evidence" for a proposition or hypothesis *h*? In asking this question, we are asking: What would be a *criterion* by means of which a particular subject S might apply our locution, "S has adequate evidence for *h*"? . . .

(1) A mark or criterion, for any subject S, that S has adequate

[1] If we wish to avoid the word "true" we may replace the locution "S accepts *h*" by "S accepts the hypothesis that *x* is *f*" or "S accepts the hypothesis that . . .;" then, instead of saying "*h* is true," we may say "*x* is *f*" or ". . . ." I have discussed the above concepts in more detail in "Epistemic Statements and the Ethics of Belief," *Philosophy and Phenomenological Research*, Vol. XVI (1956), pp. 447–460.

[2] See Sextus Empiricus, *Outlines of Pyrrhonism*, Books I and II. Cardinal Mercier described the attempts to deal with this problem as works of "criteriology"; see D. J. Mercier, *Critériologie Générale*.

evidence for a given proposition or hypothesis *h*, would be some state or condition of S which could be described without using "know," or "perceive," or "evident," or any other epistemic term. That is to say, it would be a state or condition of S which would be described in language which is "epistemically neutral."

(2) It is tempting to say that a mark for S, that S has adequate evidence for a given proposition or hypothesis *h*, would be some state or condition to which S appeals when he wishes to *show* that he has evidence for *h*—or some state or condition which he *discovers* to hold when he discovers he has adequate evidence for *h*. But the words "discover" and "show," in this present use, are themselves epistemic terms. To *discover* that some condition holds is, among other things, to acquire adequate evidence for believing that it does; and to *show* some other person that some condition holds is, among other things, to enable him to have adequate evidence for believing that it holds. If we are to formulate our second requirement in "epistemically neutral" language, I believe we must say something like this: A mark or criterion, for any subject S, that S has adequate evidence for a given proposition or hypothesis *h* would be some state or condition of S which is such that S could not make any mistake at any time about his *being* in that state or condition at that time. That is to say, S could never believe falsely at any time either that he is in that state at that time or that he is not in that state at that time.

(3) Finally, a mark or criterion, for any subject S, that S has adequate evidence for a given proposition or hypothesis *h* would be a state or condition such that, whenever S is in that state or condition, S has adequate evidence for *h*. . . .

6.

The locution, "*x* appears so-and-so to S," in one of its many senses, is used to describe one mark of evidence.

Possibly the sense of "appear" I have in mind will be suggested by the following example. Let us consider the statement: "Things which are red usually appear red (look red) in ordinary light." Among the uses of "appear red" ("look red") is one such that, in that use, the statement "Things which are red usually appear red in ordinary light" is analytic.[3] For, in this use, "appears red" may

---

[3] The term "analytic" is usually paired with the term "synthetic," as it is here. The easiest way to think of analytic statements is to treat them as definitions.

be taken to mean the same as "appears in the way that things which are red usually appear in ordinary light." But there is another use of "appears red" which is such that, in that use, the statement "Things which are red usually appear red in ordinary light" is synthetic. Using "appears red" in this second way, we could say: "There is a certain way of appearing—appearing red—which, as it happens, we have found to be the way in which red things usually appear.". . .

In the first of these two uses, the locution "appears so-and-so" functions essentially as a *comparative* locution. When we say of anything that it "appears so-and-so," in this sense, we mean to draw a comparison between the thing and things that *are* so-and-so. We mean to say something like this: "The thing appears the way you would normally expect things that are so-and-so to appear under conditions like these (or under conditions of such-and-such a sort)." But when we use "appears so-and-so" in the second of the two ways I have tried to describe, our statements are not in the same sense comparative statements; "*x* appears so-and-so," in this use, does not entail any such statement as "*x* appears the way things that are so-and-so might normally be expected to appear." Let us say that, in this second use, the locution "*x* appears so-and-so" is used *non-comparatively*.

According to my suggestion, then, the locution "*x* appears so-and-so to S," when used *non-comparatively*, describes a condition which provides S with a mark of evidence for the proposition that *x* appears so-and-so to S. If something appears blue to S (in the non-comparative sense of "appears blue"), then, in being thus "appeared to," S is in a state which provides him with a mark of evidence for the proposition that something appears blue to S.[4] Let us see whether this criterion of evidence fulfills our three conditions.

First, the ways of being "appeared to" in question can be described without using "know," or "perceive," or "evidence," or any

---

A synthetic statement is a factual statement, one which tells us something found out by experience, not asserted by definition.—Ed.

[4] Strictly speaking, a mark of evidence is described, not by "*x* appears so-and-so to S," but by "S is appeared to so-and-so, i.e., in such-and-such a way." The victim of delirium tremens, who says of an hallucinatory elephant or lizard, "That appears pink," may be right in using "pink" and wrong in thinking that *something* appears pink. But he couldn't go far wrong if he said only "I'm appeared pink to"—or, in more philosophical language, "I sense pink."

other epistemic term. And since they can be described in "epistemically neutral" language, they meet the first of our conditions.

Secondly, if a subject S is "appeared to" in one of the ways in question, then, surely, he could not believe at that time that he is not being thus "appeared to." Nor could he believe that he was being thus "appeared to" at a time when he was not being thus "appeared to." Is it possible for something to appear blue to me while I believe that nothing does, or for me to believe that something appears blue to me at a time when nothing does? (If "appears blue" were meant in its comparative sense, then we should have to say that these things are quite possible. But it is here meant in its non-comparative sense.) We could say: There are ways of appearing which are such that, for any subject S, whenever S is appeared to in one of those ways, it is false that S believes he is *not* being appeared to in that particular way; and whenever S is not being appeared to in one of those ways, it is false that S believes he *is* being appeared to in that particular way. Hence *appearing* may be said to satisfy the second of the conditions we have proposed for a mark of evidence.

And surely *appearing* satisfies the third of our conditions. Whenever anything appears in such-and-such a way to a subject S (or, better, whenever S is appeared to in such-and-such a way), then S has adequate evidence for the proposition that something is appearing to him (or, better, that he is being appeared to) in that particular way.

To be sure, no one is ever likely to *say* "I have adequate evidence for the proposition that something is appearing blue to me." But a man who is thus appeared to may use this proposition as a premise in the application of probability and induction. For example, if he happens to have adequate evidence for the proposition, "Most of the things that appear blue in this light are blue," if something now appears blue to him, and if he has adequate evidence for no other proposition bearing upon the probability of "This is blue," then he has adequate evidence for the proposition "This is blue." It is in this sense that he may be said to have adequate evidence for "Something appears blue to me."

7.

Empiricism, as an epistemological thesis, may now be defined by reference to this "appearing" criterion of evidence and to the logic of probability, or confirmation. According to empiricism in its most extreme form, the "appearing" criterion, when supplemented by the logic of probability, affords us our *only* criterion of evidence. If a subject S has adequate evidence for some statement h, then, according to this form of empiricism, either (a) h describes one of the ways S is being appeared to, in the non-comparative sense of "appear," or (b) h is a statement which is probable in relation to such non-comparative appear statements.

I think that the philosophers who have accepted this empirical thesis, or some modification of it, have been influenced by certain facts concerning the way in which we defend, or try to justify, our beliefs. But I will not discuss these facts here. Rather, I will note what seems to be one of the limitations of empiricism, as defined, and I will try to formulate an alternative thesis.

The limitation of empiricism, as defined, is that it would seem to lead us to what Hume called "scepticism with regard to the senses." For it is very difficult to think of any proposition about the "external world" which is probable—more probable than not—in relation to any set of propositions about the way in which one is appeared to. That is to say, it is very difficult to think of a set of statements of this sort: one of them is a synthetic statement, attributing some property to a material thing; the others are statements of the form, "I am appeared to in such-and-such a way," where the expression "appeared to in such-and-such a way" has what I have called its non-comparative use; and, finally, the statement about the material thing is probable—more probable than not—in relation to the statements about appearing. If there are no such sets of statements and if the empirical thesis is true, then any synthetic proposition about a material thing would be one which, for each of us, is epistemically *indifferent*—no more worthy of our confidence than is its contradictory. And if all of this were true, we might well conclude, with Hume, that "it is vain to ask, whether there be body or not?" [5]

I suggest, however, that there are other marks of evidence. One of them is described by the word "take" which occurs in our definition of "perceive." (And therefore reference to "adequate evidence" in our definition is, in a certain sense, redundant.) I shall restrict myself, in what follows, to certain comments on this additional mark of evidence.

[5] *Treatise of Human Nature,* Book I, Part IV, Section ii.

8.

What is it for a man to *take* something to have a certain characteristic—to take something to be a cat? First of all, of course, he *believes* that the thing is a cat. Secondly, the thing is appearing to him in a certain way. Thirdly, he believes (or assumes, or "takes it for granted") with respect to one of the ways he is being appeared to, that he would not now be appeared to in just that way if the thing were not a cat. (And undoubtedly he also believes, with respect to certain ways in which he might act, that if he were now to act in those ways he would be appeared to in still other cat-like ways—i.e., in ways he would not be appeared to if the thing were not a cat.) And, finally, these beliefs or assumptions were not arrived at as the result of reflection, deliberation, or inference; the man didn't weigh alternatives and then *infer* that the thing was a cat.

More generally, the locution "There is something x such that S *takes* x to be f" may be said to mean this: there is something x such that x appears in some way to S; S believes that x is f; S also believes, with respect to one of the ways he is appeared to, that he would not be appeared to in that way, under the conditions which now obtain, if x were not f; and S did not arrive at these beliefs as a result of deliberation, reflection, or inference.

If a man *takes* something to be a cat, then, as I have noted, he is not likely to *say* "I take that to be a cat." He is more likely to say "I *see* that that is a cat." [6] But the fact that he wouldn't *say* "I take that to be a cat" doesn't imply that it's false that he takes the thing to be a cat. When the King dies, his subjects do not *say* "Some public official has passed away." But the fact that they do not say it does not imply it's false that some public official has passed away.

If taking, as thus conceived, is a mark of evidence, then it must satisfy our three conditions. And I believe that it does. For (1) we have been able to say what *taking* is without using any epistemic terms; our description, or definition, does not make use of "know," "evident," "see," "perceive," or any other epistemic term. (2) No one can ever be said to believe falsely, or mistakenly, either that

---

[6] If a second man is not sure that our perceiver sees that the thing is a cat, the second man will say "He *takes* it to be a cat" or—what comes to the same thing—"He *thinks he sees* that it's a cat."

he is, or that he is not, taking something to be a cat. Of course a man may take something falsely to be a cat; i.e., he may *mis*take something for a cat. And a man may believe falsely today that yesterday he took something to be a cat. But no one can believe falsely now, with respect to himself, that he is now taking something to be a cat, or that he is not now taking something to be a cat. . . . And I suggest (3) that if a man takes something to be a cat he thereby has adequate evidence for the proposition or hypothesis that the thing *is* a cat.[7]

This theory of evidence has a kind of "internal" justification. For the hypotheses and propositions for which most of us *have* adequate evidence, if this theory is correct, indicate that most of our "takings" are true—that most of our "takings" are *perceivings*. These hypotheses and propositions indicate, as Peirce pointed out, that human beings have a tendency to make correct guesses and that the human mind is "strongly adapted to the comprehension of the world."[8]

[7] H. H. Price suggests a similar view in *Perception*, p. 185.
[8] C. S. Peirce, *Collected Papers*, 6.417.

DOUGLAS G. ARNER

Conclusive Evidence

*Douglas G. Arner (1926–) is Professor of Philosophy at Arizona
State University. He was educated at the University of Michigan, taught
at Princeton University. He is interested in ethics and theory of knowledge.*

What counts as conclusive evidence is a matter of tacit, continuing
agreement among the users of the language. We learn early that
we are not to claim knowledge unless we have met certain requirements in the way of qualifications and evidence. These requirements
are founded chiefly on what grounds have proved adequate almost
all of the time. Not exactly all the time; considerations of con-
venience have a place. In a trial, everything that is logically relevant
is not a subject for inquiry. Some things are simply noticed judicially,
others admitted; in general, inquiry goes only to what can be
doubted. It is much the same in the ordinary course of allaying
doubt. There must be a stop to investigation and to taking measures
against the chance of error. We want always to be correct but
not at the price of endless checking and hedging. Considerations
of reliability are always of the first importance, of course. In some
areas the best available evidence is not enough and there we speak
of matters of opinion, subjects for conjecture. But to mark something as a matter of opinion is only a different way of putting a stop
to inquiry. It is impossible to say in general what counts as conclusive evidence, for it depends on the subject matter and circumstances, and it depends on these in different ways. But I do not
regard each sunrise as confirming anything nor do I check my
color vision on the hour, yet it is not just very probable that the
sun will rise tomorrow or that this pencil is red.

It is quite true that grounds treated as conclusive are always
short of a demonstration and even occasionally prove inadequate.
This is not important. The important thing is that conclusive

From Douglas G. Arner, "On Knowing," *The Philosophical Review*, **LXVIII**,
No. 1 (January 1959), Sec. 5. Reprinted by permission of the Editorial Board
of *The Philosophical Review* and the author.

evidence *concludes:* no demand for more evidence in the face of conclusive evidence is intelligible.

Stating evidence must be distinguished from stating reasons, premises, assumptions, as demanding proof or evidence must be distinguished from simply inquiring about another's reasons. We may ask that someone give us some grounds to accept what he said or we may ask what led him to say what he said. The latter query need not witness a refusal to concede what was said. Similarly, we will not allow that someone has produced evidence unless he has cited facts, spoken the truth; but he may, in stating his reasons, premises, assumptions, state what is not fact but mere opinion or conjecture. The point is that to describe someone as having stated or produced evidence is to allow, among other things, that he has kept to the truth. Thus one cannot without absurdity demand evidence for evidence or speak of evidence as false.

Whenever anyone asserts anything, there is an ostensible basis for others to accept what he says. (There is at least his testimony.) A demand for evidence, a refusal to allow the matter on that basis, implies that one cannot concede, grant, allow this kind of thing on this kind of basis. Thus there is implicit in every such demand a restriction on what may be produced as evidence: nothing will be treated as evidence which is not itself more firmly grounded than the original matter. Now if the ostensible basis for an assertion amounts to conclusive evidence, a demand for more evidence is self-nullifying. "If this will not be conceded, what can be?" Giving evidence is a matter of citing authorities, stating facts, and performing tests. But authorities, facts, and tests are necessarily accepted, well-known, and acknowledged. Such queries remove the background against which evidence is demanded and produced, for that background is founded on nothing better than conclusive evidence. "If he demands proof for this, whom must he count as an authority, what can he take as plain, which tests will he regard as effective?"

Of course, some apparently unintelligible demands may prove to be merely exotic. Explanation may show that the circumstances are in some way special or the ostensible basis not what it seemed. In philosophy, the existence of one's hands, desk, and ink bottle tend to become subjects of investigation. Such demands are utterly self-nullifying: the ostensible basis is so extensive that asking for evidence, for something one can allow, witnesses that nothing can be allowed. Such demands cannot be retrieved by an explanation. That the evidence available is not logically conclusive, or that others have been mistaken in the same situation, does not provide a warrant for such inquiries. (You can always say that.) As I cannot get evidence, I cannot even have reasons for saying that my hand or desk or ink bottle exists, for nothing could be better established. There is a temptation to say that I have the best of reasons— somehow my whole life, everything, stands behind these truths. The source of this temptation is the fact that if I am not to concede such things, I can concede nothing. This is why no one can sensibly wonder if he is dreaming or is hallucinated when all appears normal. That is to "question" the plainest things. What could he count as evidence that he was dreaming? Or that he was not?

"Know" is used to assure others in a special way. It indicates that the evidence is not merely good but is as good as can be, that further investigation has lost its point. "Know" closes questions, stops debates. Allowing that someone knows or knew something is incompatible with continued inquiry and caution. This is what constitutes the gravity of the claim: in authorizing others to consider matters closed, I assume a special responsibility for the consequences of error. It is in this way that the difference between "know" and "probable" is to be understood. When we say that S is P is probable, we are liable to support our claim by showing, say, that in this kind of situation S has been P more often than not. If experience to date does reveal this, then whatever happens, it was probable that S was P. This is the point of saying that probability is relative to evidence. When we say we know, we are liable to show that experience to date makes unintelligible a demand for more evidence. Now further experience cannot change what experience showed at some previous time but it can reopen closed questions and renew old debates. It commonly happens that what at some previous time could not sensibly have been questioned comes, in the light of subsequent events, into question. At some times and places a demand for proof that the earth was round would not have been intelligible. If "know" merely signaled evidence of a certain weight, we could allow that people knew even if they have proved wrong. But "know" signals conclusive evidence which is not, as it were, a matter of the timeless weight of evidence. If further experience has reopened a question or disposed of it in a different way, we cannot allow that someone knew, though the evidence in hand at the time of the claim was as good as could be. Hence, in denying that someone knew, we are not necessarily denying the propriety of the claim. To say we know when we do not even think we know is improper; it is only a mistake to say we know when we merely think we know.

Scepticism

There is a species of scepticism, *antecedent* to all study and philosophy, which is much inculcated by Des Cartes and others, as a sovereign preservative against error and precipitate judgement. It recommends an universal doubt, not only of all our former opinions and principles, but also of our very faculties; of whose veracity, say they, we must assure ourselves, by a chain of reasoning, deduced from some original principle, which cannot possibly be fallacious or deceitful. But neither is there any such original principle, which has a prerogative above others, that are self-evident and convincing: or if there were, could we advance a step beyond it, but by the use of those very faculties, of which we are supposed to be already diffident. The Cartesian doubt, therefore, were it ever possible to be attained by any human creature (as it plainly is not) would be entirely incurable; and no reasoning could ever bring us to a state of assurance and conviction upon any subject.

It must, however, be confessed, that this species of scepticism, when more moderate, may be understood in a very reasonable sense, and is a necessary preparative to the study of philosophy, by preserving a proper impartiality in our judgements, and weaning our mind from all those prejudices, which we may have imbibed from education or rash opinion. To begin with clear and self-evident principles, to advance by timorous and sure steps, to review frequently our conclusions, and examine accurately all their consequences; though by these means we shall make both a slow and a short progress in our systems; are the only methods, by which we can ever hope to reach truth, and attain a proper stability and certainty in our determinations.

There is another species of scepticism, *consequent* to science and enquiry, when men are supposed to have discovered, either the absolute fallaciousness of their mental faculties, or their unfitness to reach any fixed determination in all those curious subjects of speculation, about which they are commonly employed. Even our very senses are brought into dispute, by a certain species of philosophers; and the maxims of common life are subjected to the same

Hume, *op. cit.*, Sec. XII, Parts I, II, III, pp. 149–164, *passim.*

doubt as the most profound principles or conclusions of metaphysics and theology. As these paradoxical tenets (if they may be called tenets) are to be met with in some philosophers, and the refutation of them in several, they naturally excite our curiosity, and make us enquire into the arguments, on which they may be founded.

I need not insist upon the more trite topics, employed by the sceptics in all ages, against the evidence of *sense;* such as those which are derived from the imperfection and fallaciousness of our organs, on numberless occasions; the crooked appearance of an oar in water; the various aspects of objects, according to their different distances; the double images which arise from the pressing one eye; with many other appearances of a like nature. These sceptical topics, indeed, are only sufficient to prove, that the senses alone are not implicitly to be depended on; but that we must correct their evidence by reason, and by considerations, derived from the nature of the medium, the distance of the object, and the disposition of the organ, in order to render them, within their sphere, the proper *criteria* of truth and falsehood. There are other more profound arguments against the senses, which admit not of so easy a solution.

It seems evident, that men are carried, by a natural instinct or prepossession, to repose faith in their senses; and that, without any reasoning, or even almost before the use of reason, we always suppose an external universe, which depends not on our perception, but would exist, though we and every sensible creature were absent or annihilated. Even the animal creations are governed by a like opinion, and preserve this belief of external objects, in all their thoughts, designs, and actions.

It seems also evident, that, when men follow this blind and powerful instinct of nature, they always suppose the very images, presented by the senses, to be the external objects, and never entertain any suspicion, that the one are nothing but representations of the other. This very table, which we see white, and which we feel hard, is believed to exist, independent of our perception, and to be something external to our mind, which perceives it. Our presence bestows not being on it: our absence does not annihilate it. It preserves its existence uniform and entire, independent of the situation of intelligent beings, who perceive or contemplate it.

But this universal and primary opinion of all men is soon destroyed by the slightest philosophy, which teaches us, that nothing can ever be present to the mind but an image or perception, and that the senses are only the inlets, through which these images are conveyed, without being able to produce any immediate intercourse between the mind and the object. The table, which we see, seems to diminish, as we remove farther from it: but the real table, which exists independent of us, suffers no alteration: it was, therefore, nothing but its image, which was present to the mind. These are the obvious dictates of reason; and no man, who reflects, ever doubted, that the existences, which we consider, when we say, *this house* and *that tree*, are nothing but perceptions in the mind, and fleeting copies or representations of other existences, which remain uniform and independent.

So far, then, are we necessitated by reasoning to contradict or depart from the primary instincts of nature, and to embrace a new system with regard to the evidence of our senses. But here philosophy finds herself extremely embarrassed, when she would justify this new system, and obviate the cavils and objections of the sceptics. She can no longer plead the infallible and irresistible instinct of nature: for that led us to a quite different system, which is acknowledged fallible and even erroneous. And to justify this pretended philosophical system, by a chain of clear and convincing argument, or even any appearance of argument, exceeds the power of all human capacity.

By what argument can it be proved, that the perceptions of the mind must be caused by external objects, entirely different from them, though resembling them (if that be possible) and could not arise either from the energy of the mind itself, or from the suggestion of some invisible and unknown spirit, or from some other cause still more unknown to us? It is acknowledged, that, in fact, many of these perceptions arise not from anything external, as in dreams, madness, and other diseases. And nothing can be more inexplicable than the manner, in which body should so operate upon mind as ever to convey an image of itself to a substance, supposed of so different, and even contrary a nature.

It is a question of fact, whether the perceptions of the senses be produced by external objects, resembling them: how shall this question be determined? By experience surely; as all other questions of a like nature. But here experience is, and must be entirely silent. The mind has never anything present to it but the perceptions, and cannot possibly reach any experience of their connexion with objects. The supposition of such a connexion is, therefore, without any foundation in reasoning. . . .

Thus the first philosophical objection to the evidence of sense or to the opinion of external existence consists in this, that such an opinion, if rested on natural instinct, is contrary to reason, and if referred to reason, is contrary to natural instinct, and at the same time carries no rational evidence with it, to convince an impartial enquirer. The second objection goes farther, and represents this opinion as contrary to reason: at least, if it be a principle of reason, that all sensible qualities are in the mind, not in the object. Bereave matter of all its intelligible qualities, both primary and secondary, you in a manner annihilate it, and leave only a certain unknown, inexplicable *something*, as the cause of our perceptions; a notion so imperfect, that no sceptic will think it worth while to contend against it. . . .

It is needless to insist farther on this head. These objections are but weak. For as, in common life, we reason every moment concerning fact and existence, and cannot possibly subsist, without continually employing this species of argument, any popular objections, derived from thence, must be insufficient to destroy that evidence. The great subverter of *Pyrrhonism* or the excessive principles of scepticism is action, and employment, and the occupations of common life. These principles may flourish and triumph in the schools; where it is, indeed, difficult, if not impossible, to refute them. But as soon as they leave the shade, and by the presence of the real objects, which actuate our passions and sentiments, are put in opposition to the more powerful principles of our nature, they vanish like smoke, and leave the most determined sceptic in the same condition as other mortals.

The sceptic, therefore, had better keep within his proper sphere, and display those *philosophical* objections, which arise from more profound researches. Here he seems to have ample matter of triumph; while he justly insists, that all our evidence for any matter of fact, which lies beyond the testimony of sense or memory, is derived entirely from the relation of cause and effect; that we have no other idea of this relation than that of two objects, which have been frequently *conjoined* together; that we have no argument to convince us, that objects, which have, in our experience, been frequently conjoined, will likewise, in other instances, be conjoined in the same manner; and that nothing leads us to this inference but custom or a certain instinct of our nature; which it is indeed difficult to resist, but which, like other instincts, may be fallacious and deceitful. While the sceptic insists upon these topics, he shows his force, or rather, indeed, his own and our weakness; and seems, arguments might be displayed at greater length, if any durable for the time at least, to destroy all assurance and conviction. These good or benefit to society could ever be expected to result from them.

For here is the chief and most confounding objections to *excessive* scepticism, that no durable good can ever result from it; while it remains in its full force and vigour . . . A Pyrrhonian cannot expect, that his philosophy will have any constant influence on the mind: or if it had, that its influence would be beneficial to society. On the contrary, he must acknowledge, if he will acknowledge anything, that all human life must perish, were his principles universally and steadily to prevail. All discourse, all action would immediately cease; and men remain in a total lethargy, till the necessities of nature, unsatisfied, put an end to their miserable existence. . . .

There is, indeed, a more *mitigated* scepticism or *academical* philosophy, which may be both durable and useful, and which may, in part, be the result of this Pyrrhonism, or *excessive* scepticism, when its undistinguished doubts are, in some measure, corrected by common sense and reflection. The greater part of mankind are naturally apt to be affirmative and dogmatical in their opinions; and while they see objects only on one side, and have no idea of any counterpoising argument, they throw themselves precipitately into the principles, to which they are inclined; nor have they any indulgence for those who entertain opposite sentiments. To hesitate or balance perplexes their understanding, checks their passion, and suspends their action. They are, therefore, impatient till they escape from a state, which to them is so uneasy: and they think, that they could never remove themselves far enough from it, by the violence of their affirmations and obstinacy of their belief. But could such dogmatical reasoners become sensible of the strange infirmities of human understanding, even in its most perfect state, and when most accurate and cautious in its determinations; such a reflection would naturally inspire them with more modesty and reserve, and diminish their fond opinion of themselves, and their prejudice against antagonists. . . .

Another species of *mitigated* scepticism which may be of advantage to mankind, and which may be the natural result of the Pyrrhonian doubts and scruples, is the limitation of our enquiries to such subjects as are best adapted to the narrow capacity of human understanding. The *imagination* of man is naturally sublime, delighted with whatever is remote and extraordinary, and running, without control, into the most distant parts of space and time in order to avoid the objects, which custom has rendered too familiar to it. A correct *Judgement* observes a contrary method, and avoiding all distant and high enquiries, confines itself to common life, and to such subjects as fall under daily practice and experience; leaving the more sublime topics to the embellishment of poets and orators, or to the arts of priests and politicians. To bring us to so salutary a determination, nothing can be more serviceable, than to be once thoroughly convinced of the force of the Pyrrhonian doubt, and of the impossibility, that anything, but the strong power of natural instinct, could free us from it. Those who have a propensity to philosophy, will still continue their researches; because they reflect, that, besides the immediate pleasure, attending such an occupation, philosophical decisions are nothing but the reflections of common life, methodized and corrected. But they will never be tempted to go beyond common life, so long as they consider the imperfection of those faculties which they employ, their narrow reach, and their inaccurate operations.

Bibliography

The reader is urged to explore further in the works represented in this anthology. Books and articles cited in the footnotes of the readings are recommended for further study. Two general books on theory of knowledge which can be consulted with profit are the following:

A. J. Ayer. *The Problem of Knowledge* (Baltimore: Penguin, 1956).
A. D. Woozley. *Theory of Knowledge* (London: Hutchinson Univ. Library, 1949).

The following are a few additional sources for further readings in the three areas of this anthology.

PART I. DESCRIPTIVE EPISTEMOLOGY

Cassirer, Ernst. *The Philosophy of Symbolic Forms,* Vol. I (New Haven: Yale Univ. Press, 1953).

Piaget, Jean. *The Child's Conception of Reality* (London: Routledge, 1955).

Merleau-Ponty, M. *Phenomenology of Perception* (London: Routledge, 1962).

Santayana, George. *Reason in Common Sense,* Chap. I (New York: Scribner, 1934 [or in the one-volume edition, *The Life of Reason,* 1953]).

Whitely, C. H. "On Understanding," *Mind,* **LVIII** (1949).

Yolton, John W. *Thinking and Perceiving* (La Salle, Ill.: Open Court, 1962).

PART II. SOME FORMS OF COGNITION

Austin, J. L. *Sense and Sensibilia* (Oxford: Clarendon, 1962).

Benjamin, B. S. "Remembering," *Mind,* **LXV** (1956).

Butler, R. J. "Other Dates," *Mind,* **LXVIII** (1959).

Furlong, E. J. "Memory," *Mind,* **LVII** (1948).

Malcolm, N. "Knowledge and Belief," *Mind,* **LXI** (1952).

Saunders, J. T. "Skepticism and Memory," *The Philosophical Review,* **LXXII** (1963).

Price, H. H. *Perception* (London: Methuen, 1932).

Will, F. L. "Justification and Induction," *The Philosophical Review,* **LXVIII** (1959).

PART III. NORMATIVE EPISTEMOLOGY

Firth, R. "Chisholm and the Ethics of Belief," *The Philosophical Review,* **LXVIII** (1959).

Husserl, Edmund. *Cartesian Meditations* (The Hague: Nijhoff, 1960).

Harrison, J. "Knowing and Promising," *Mind,* **LXXI** (1962).

Thomas, L. E. "Philosophic Doubt," *Mind,* **LXIV** (1955).

Urmson, J. O. "On Grading," *Mind,* **LIX** (1950).

Wellman, C. "Wittgenstein's Conception of a Criterion," *The Philosophical Review,* **LXXI** (1962).